CONTENTS

WELCOME

Right Rev Dr Derek Browning
Moderator of the General Assembly of the Church of Scotland

Sister Wendy Beckett, Carmelite nun and art critic, wrote recently:

> Unless we understand our faith we cannot live it, but it is the living that matters. Knowing and thinking and understanding are all means to draw us into the life of Christ, an active living and loving way of being. Christianity is both simple and profound.[1]

One of the joys of faith is the questing and the enquiring, and the delight of knowing that the God we worship relishes our questions and sees them as a true sign of lively faith within us. Asking questions about faith, what we believe, why we believe and how we believe is not the sole preserve of the rarefied academic theologian. It is the spiritual heritage and, dare I say, property of every child of God who has ever asked the question, 'Why?' I believe that much of the Bible was written with this very question in mind, and the fact that so many answers are given shows that Christian faith, imaginatively lived, is an evolving, dynamic and supple experience.

During the 1988 General Assembly I remember a speaker talking about the need to offer greater theological education and opportunity to the people in the pews. The Church was challenged to admit the fact that instead of creating giants of faith, we had colluded in the creation of spiritual pygmies. In many cases that is far from the reality, but I wonder if there remains some element of truth to the challenge. When people are afraid to ask questions about their faith and their doubts, the Church has work to do. Faith is a questing thing and it is meant to ask many questions. A faith that does not ask questions will be shallow. A faith that thinks it knows all the answers is going to be in for a surprise. Enquiring minds, applying lived-out faith to daily life, making connections and drawing conclusions, and exploring the familiar and unfamiliar territories of the Kingdom of God is a noble aspiration for our Church today.

In the eleventh century St Anselm, a Benedictine monk, philosopher, theologian and Archbishop of Canterbury, wondered how to explain the existence of God. Some scholars suggest that this man should have had as his motto, *fides quaerens intellectum* – 'faith seeking understanding'.

It gives me great pleasure to commend to you this latest addition to the excellent *Learn* series. Read it, question it, find help within it, challenge it and share it. I hope your faith continues seeking understanding. ■

1. Endorsement for Rowan Williams, *Being Christian* (London: SPCK, 2014), inside cover.

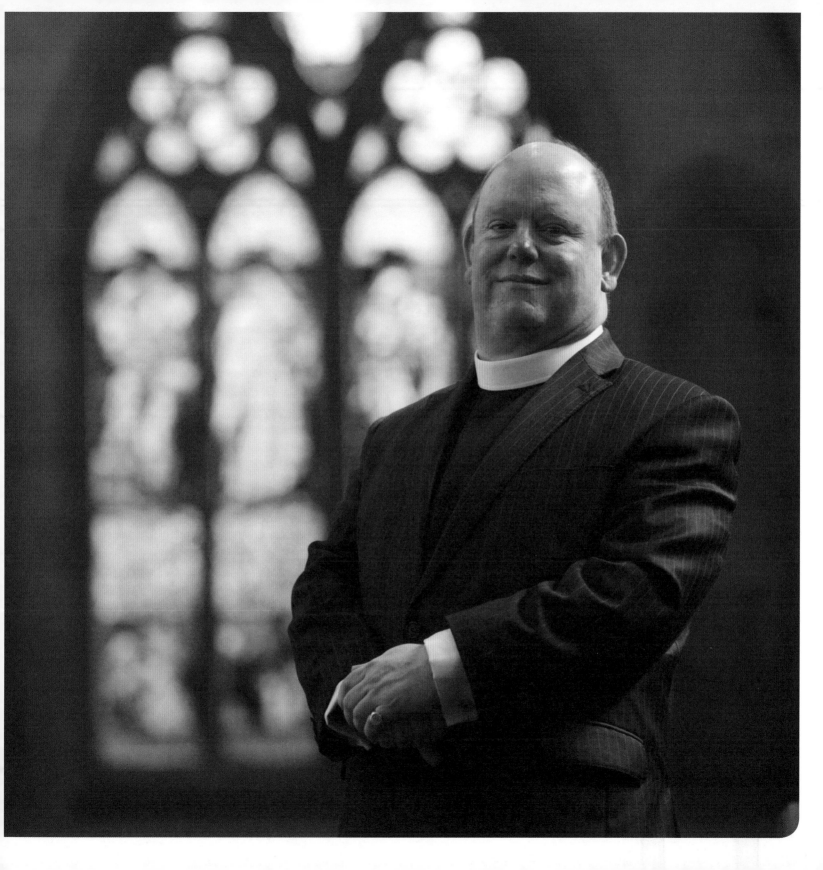

KNOWING GOD

Bible Study: Alison Jack

Reflection: Frances Henderson

Prayer: David D. Scott

BIBLE STUDY

'Lord, show us the Father, and we will be satisfied'
John 14.8

Genesis 32.22–32
John 14.7–14

'How can we know God?' is a question that several characters in the Bible struggle to answer.

In the Old Testament, the story of Jacob wrestling with the mysterious figure in the dead of night is a powerful metaphor for this struggle. The setting is one of anxiety: Jacob is returning to meet his brother Esau, whom he cheated out of his birthright. He is alone in the dark, at a crossing point. Suddenly, out of nowhere a man assaults him, and they struggle through the night. Jacob demands a blessing, but in response the man gives him a new name to reflect the significance of Jacob's struggle. The man refuses to reveal his own name, but blesses Jacob, who now understands that he has indeed had an encounter with God himself. Read Genesis 32.22–32 and consider the ways in which the story refuses to give clear answers about what is happening. Why is Jacob so certain he has met with God by the end, and why does the story suggest that it matters?

In the New Testament, John's Gospel explores the revelation of who God is in some depth. By opening with the statement that 'In the beginning was the Word, and the Word was with God, and the Word was God', John is suggesting something very profound about God and the way God reveals Godself to creation. The term 'Word' is a translation of a Greek word, *logos*, which had a wide range of meaning. For Greek and Roman philosophers, it could refer to the rational principle that governed the universe; in a Jewish context, it was used to define the creative plan of God for the world. It takes us back to the first creation story in Genesis, and to God's speaking the world into existence: 'And God said ...' It is through the Word that God comes to be known and God's presence is felt in creation. By associating Jesus with the Word, John gives him a profound significance in terms of his role in revealing the nature of God in the world – from the beginning of time to the period of his ministry on earth, and beyond.

Perhaps to encourage those of us who continue to find this hard, John also presents the example of the disciples as they struggle to make sense of the role of Jesus in embodying God in the world. Read John 14.7–14 and consider how Jesus responds to Philip's request to see the Father. In what ways might Jesus' answer satisfy Philip's demand? What might be the 'works' to which Jesus refers? Note the invitation Jesus gives here to participate in the revelatory works of Jesus and the Father. The Word invites a relationship of trust and participation, not just the agreement of our minds.

What do we know about God?

In the history of Christian thought, much time has been spent reflecting upon the different ways in which we might come to know God and to have knowledge of God. A number of different lines of thinking have been suggested, and we can gather these under three headings: negative theology, natural theology, and revealed theology. Each one is considered in turn.

Negative theology

A first way of answering the question of what we know about God would be given by 'negative theology'. The starting-point of this way of thinking is the view that God is so far outside our human understanding and experience that the best we can do in describing God is to say what God is *not*. As the old hymn puts it, God is 'immortal, invisible … unresting, unhasting', and so on. Notice how these are all negative words. Humans are mortal and visible; but all we can say about God is that God is not what we are.

There is a very important insight here. The Bible often reminds us that God is beyond human perception. The psalmist writes that the knowledge of God is 'too wonderful for me; it is so high that I cannot attain it' (Psalm 139.6). Paul comments on 'How unsearchable are [God's] judgements and how inscrutable his ways!' (Romans 11.33). We remind ourselves finally of the second commandment: 'You shall not make for yourself an idol' (Exodus 20.4). Just as God cannot be contained by depictions in clay or paint, so neither can God be contained by words – we can never truly comprehend God.

For this reason, negative theology is a useful place to start when we ask what we know about God. Even when we think we have gained an insight into God, we should remember that, because of our sin, we are very good at making our own 'graven images' of God: idols or fantasies built from over-extended analogies, childhood misconceptions and wishful thinking. Negative theology can help us to clear out our preconceptions, and repent of them before a God who is greater than we can ever conceive.

Natural theology

A second way of answering the question of what we know about God offers a different, more positive route forward. True, God is immortal and invisible – but God has created this mortal and visible world, and God has also given us the faculty of reason, expecting that we will use it. So some Christians believe that there is

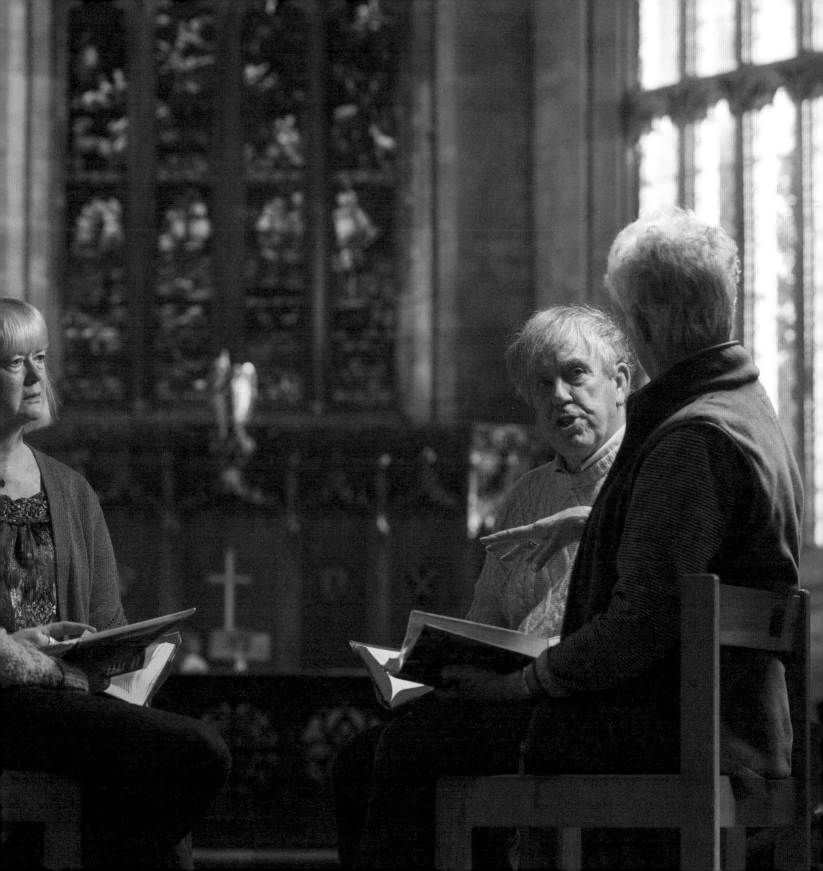

implanted in human nature some knowledge or awareness or inclination related to God. And some Christians believe that we should be able to look at the world around us, at its order and its purpose and its beauty, and on that basis be able to know that God exists and to know something of the character of God. These views are representative of what is called 'natural theology'.

In the Bible, Paul seems to support the view that there is a kind of innate or natural knowledge of God when he writes that 'Ever since the creation of the world his eternal power and divine nature, invisible though they are, have been understood and seen through the things he has made' (Romans 1.20). Paul also suggests to the people in Athens that God has arranged the world in such a way that people 'would search for God and perhaps grope for him and find him – though indeed he is not far from each one of us' (Acts 17.27). Although the Athenians were neither Jews nor Christians, Paul seems to think that some knowledge of God was available to them through their own experience of and in this world.

There are many varieties of natural theology, but common to them all is the view that natural knowledge of God does not presuppose any fully developed Christian faith. Natural theology therefore has its limits, and does not try to explain any of the mysteries of Christian faith such as the incarnation. For the believer, then, there should be no contradiction between this natural knowledge of God and faith; instead, the two should complement each other, agreeing where their claims coincide.

Revealed theology

The problem with natural theology, however, may be that in the end the gulf between creation and Creator is simply too great to be overcome by our natural abilities or efforts. This would hold true even if the world had not fallen, and our minds were not corrupted by sin. And so some Christians believe that we are simply so different from God that gaining knowledge of God may be impossible from our side, no matter how brilliant our human reason, how uplifting our human experience, or how glorious the divine creation.

This has been a prominent line of Christian thought in the twentieth century, with a growing suspicion of knowledge of God based simply on human understanding or experience and an increasing emphasis on the radical difference between God and humanity. The result is to suggest that if we have any knowledge of God at all, it can only be because God in mercy has crossed the divide and 'come down' to us. And God has accomplished precisely such a

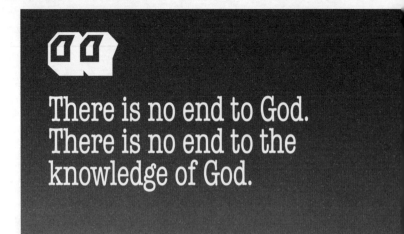

There is no end to God. There is no end to the knowledge of God.

merciful 'coming down' by revealing Godself to the people of God in Scripture and in Jesus Christ. The resultant knowledge of God is 'revealed theology'.

There are certain Christian truths that have always been understood to be 'revealed' to believers. One of these is knowledge of the Trinity, that God is One, and that God is also three Persons – Father, Son and Spirit. Another revealed truth is the incarnation, in which 'the Word became flesh and lived among us' (John 1.14). That God is Trinity and that Jesus is the Word incarnate are not truths of logic or truths we could have known or discovered by ourselves. Instead, they are truths we know only because they have been revealed to us directly by God through the Word and the Spirit, as Scripture attests.

The question, then, about how we can know God and what we can know about God, is answered most directly by pointing to Jesus. Jesus himself tells us that 'Whoever has seen me has seen the Father' (John 14.9). While he lived and preached on earth, the disciples caught glimpses of this divine glory in him. But it was not until his resurrection that they were at last confronted directly with the glory of God. It is then that Thomas finally sees who Jesus truly is, and makes his great confession: 'My Lord and my God' (John 20.28). This same confession is made now by all who meet Jesus through the pages of Scripture and the witness of the Church, as the Spirit enables them to see God in him.

The revelation of the Word of God in Jesus Christ and in the Bible means that we can talk about God not only in negative terms, but also in positive words. If Jesus was angry at injustice, we can say that God is angry at injustice. If Jesus was forgiving, we can say that God is forgiving. If Jesus was humble, vulnerable and self-sacrificing, then we can say that God is humble, vulnerable and self-sacrificing. Some of these latter qualities in particular are not the kind of qualities we usually associate with our idea of what a god is. We only know they are true of God because they are true of Jesus. And as Jesus said, 'If you know me, you will know my Father also' (John 14.7). There is no more complete knowledge of God than this.

A word of caution

There is a final word of caution on this subject. Knowing fully, 'even as [we] have been fully known' (1 Corinthians 13.12), is a situation that Scripture tells us belongs to the future. Even those who know God in Jesus cannot claim full knowledge of every aspect of God's being or will. We are too little and too broken to grasp the whole of God. We have grasped perhaps only the tiniest part, though even that tiny part is more than enough and vast beyond imagining. And in eternity, even when we know fully, there will still be the continuously unfolding joys of *who God is*, new every morning for us, to discover and rediscover. There is no end to God. There is no end to the knowledge of God.

the Bible ... is the sole and primary judge for all the claims of the Christian faith

Why should we read the Bible?

The God of the Bible

As we saw when we considered 'revealed theology', Jesus Christ is for Christians the primary revelation of God. Through his words and deeds, we are given an astonishing insight into the very being of God. So if we want to know God, then we have to begin with knowing Jesus.

But when it comes down to it, only Jesus' first disciples had the privilege of knowing him in person. For the rest of us, living in a different time and place, we have to rely on their written accounts. This is not in itself a disadvantage – Jesus tells Thomas that there is a special blessing for those 'who have not seen and yet have come to believe' (John 20.29). But it does mean that our route to faith is a little different from that of the first disciples. We do not get to know Jesus in the flesh, as they did. Instead, we modern-day disciples come to know Jesus principally through the Bible.

At this most fundamental level, then, we need Scripture. The Bible is the primary and basic access we have to Jesus. Of course, we might say that we can know Jesus in other ways. In particular, Christians claim a personal relationship with Jesus, and speak of knowing Jesus in their hearts. All of this is true, and all of this is the work of the Spirit. But we can only be sure that we are encountering *Jesus* – and not our own imagination – by referring back to the message of the Bible. It is the Bible that is the sole and primary judge for all the claims of the Christian faith – this is the basic meaning of the phrase 'Scripture alone', which was so important to the Protestant Reformers.

Of course, God was speaking through Scripture long before Jesus was born. With Judaism, Christianity believes that God has spoken through the Law and through the prophets. Moreover, the story of God and of the people of God is told all the way through the Bible, from the beginning of creation to the end of time. Because of this story, and the particular content of this story, we cannot think of God in abstract terms as a 'higher power' – rather, the God of the Bible is the God of Abraham, Isaac and Jacob. So when Jesus claimed to reveal God the Father, it is this personal God of the Old Testament that he reveals.

One Bible, two Testaments

Throughout Christian history, believers have puzzled over how best to understand the relationship between the Old Testament and the New Testament. Some Christians tend to think that the Old Testament is about 'Law', while the New Testament is about 'Grace', and believe that Grace has simply replaced the Law such that the Old Testament is no longer valid. Nowadays, however, Christians tend to be very cautious about this 'replacement' theory: it gives a false understanding of Judaism as a graceless religion, and has historically contributed to the Christian persecution of the Jews.

From its early days, guided by John Calvin and John Knox, the Church of Scotland has regarded both Testaments as necessary for the knowledge of God and our salvation. The grace and promise of the New Testament is already present in the witness of the Old Testament, while the laws set forth in the Old Testament find an echo in the commands and guidance of the New Testament.

Nevertheless, it is certainly the case that Jesus is so central for Christians that the teaching about him in the New Testament holds a privileged place. Not only does the New Testament tell us about Jesus, but it also serves as a lens through which to read the Old Testament. So, for example, Christians will read the story of manna being given to the people of Israel in the desert (Exodus

> ## " The writers of the New Testament ... understand Jesus as the ultimate validation of the truth of the Old Testament.

16.31), and make the connection with Jesus as the bread of life (John 6.35). The writers of the New Testament explicitly encourage these connections, and understand Jesus as the ultimate validation of the truth of the Old Testament.

How do we know the Bible is true?

When talking about the truth of the Bible, there are three key words that are often used: *inspired*, *infallible* and *inerrant*. They are related words, but they each mean slightly different things.

Inspired means 'breathed', or 'God-breathed' (cf. 2 Timothy 3.16). It means that Scripture has been written under the direct influence of the Spirit, so

that God is in some way the author of the Bible. It is often held to follow as a consequence that Scripture is *infallible* – meaning that it cannot be wrong or contradict itself, any more than God can. And this in turn is often understood to mean that Scripture must be *inerrant* – without error, and thus perfect as God's knowledge is perfect.

However, the truthfulness of the Bible is perceived by others to be not quite as simple as that. Although Christians generally believe that God inspired Scripture, it is certainly not the case that God dictated the text to writers who were working in some kind of robotic trance. The prophets and apostles who wrote the text were real people, people of a particular time and a particular culture. We can perhaps see the limits of their understanding when we read the creation accounts, and even beyond matters of science, our knowledge and view of the world changes over time. Even within Scripture itself, we can discern developments in the attitudes displayed towards women, marriage, kings, foreigners, even God.

Moreover, the Bible was composed by many different people. For example, scholars believe that the two accounts of creation in the early chapters of Genesis were written by different authors, describing events rather differently. Yet it is not necessary to go through all sorts of mental gymnastics to bring the two chapters to harmony: both have something vital to say about God, and so the ancient editors of Genesis seem to have been content to live with the tension. In this, they may have demonstrated much wisdom.

A further issue is language. We know that our Bibles have been translated from the original Hebrew and Greek into English. The result is a loss of many of the nuances of the original. Our words are 'loaded' with associations and preconceptions, so that translation is never as simple as matching a Hebrew word with an English one, but already includes a layer of interpretation on the part of the translator. And we must also realise that language itself is human and sinful, as the episode of the Tower of Babel suggests (Genesis 11.9) – there is simply no 'pure' earthly language for God to use when speaking to us. In every case, then, God accommodates the divine message to our human means and capabilities.

Of course, none of this means that Scripture is not inspired, infallible or inerrant. But in practice it means that we do have to think very carefully about what we mean by these words, and about how we handle the text of Scripture with appropriate care, understanding and modesty.

How do we know we are reading Scripture correctly?

Reading the Bible is both simple and more complicated than we think. The simple part is the belief that God speaks to us through Scripture, which points towards Jesus. We believe this because we have been convinced by the same Spirit who inspired Scripture in the first place. It is this conviction by the Spirit that alone enables us to affirm 'the Word of God, which is contained in the Scriptures of the Old and New Testaments, to be the supreme rule of faith and life'.[1] That is the simple part.

The complicated part is us. We are fallible and errant readers of a book written by all-too-human scribes. We must therefore approach the reading of Scripture prayerfully, remembering that 'without the illumination of the Spirit the Word has no effect'.[2] We must be willing to enter imaginatively into a world very different from our own, and be open to the work of scholars who have studied these texts and these times. And above all, we must read Scripture with the constant and humbling remembrance that it is God who is inspired, infallible and inerrant, and not our interpretation of the Word of God.

All this might be less clear than we would like. Interpretation would be a whole lot easier if the Bible did indeed read more like a rule book for life, and less like a winding, playful, occasionally contradictory grand epic. Nevertheless, it may yet console us that the incarnation suggests that God is used to speaking through human mess and muddle, and is more than capable of making the best of it.

1. **First Article Declaratory of the Constitution of the Church of Scotland**, at www.churchofscotland.org.uk/about_us/church_law/church_constitution (accessed 1 May 2017).
2. John Calvin, *Institutes of the Christian Religion* (Louisville, KY: WJKP, 2006), III.ii.33.

QUESTIONS

1. Consider the pictures of God that you have carried in your head, perhaps from childhood onwards – where do they come from, and how helpful or unhelpful might they be in thinking about God?

2. What (if anything) can we tell about God and God's plan for us by looking at the world around us, and can scientific knowledge about the world help us understand God better?

3. The Bible is our 'supreme rule of faith and life', but does not mention many issues of current concern, from nuclear weapons to stem-cell research ... so how can the Bible guide us on these matters today?

Almighty God,
out of the silence of eternity
You have given us Your Word.
Out of the silence of the womb
You have given us Your Son.
Out of the silence of prayer
You have given us Your Spirit.
For the Word
contained in the Old and New Testaments
reflecting Your love for the creation and Your new
creation;
for the Word made flesh
celebrating Your supreme communication
with people in all ages and all places;
for the Word of life and love
enlightening our minds and hearts
in words of wisdom and mercy
and acts of goodness and grace –
we give You thanks!
Let Your living Word
dwell in us richly
that we may live to build and not destroy,
to seek peace and not disunity,
to sacrifice our interpretation of the truth
for the One who is the Truth.
Above all,
teach us
when to fill the silence with our words
and when our words should not be spoken;
for it is only through this wisdom
that the things we say
and the things we don't say
will speak about Your living Word,
even Jesus Christ, our Saviour and Lord.

GOD THE CREATOR

Bible Study: **Alison Jack**

Reflection: **David Fergusson**

Prayer: **David D. Scott**

BIBLE STUDY

'O Lord, our sovereign, how majestic is your name in all the earth!'
Psalm 8.9

Genesis 1—3
Psalm 8
Revelation 21.1—6 and 22.1—5
Hebrews 1.1—4 and 2.5—9

A psalm such as Psalm 8 may be read as a response of praise to the story of creation outlined in Genesis 1—2. The psalm speaks of order and defined roles for all aspects of the created world, both in their relationship to God and in their relationships to each other. A hierarchy is firmly established which places God, humanity and the other creatures of the earth, sea and air in descending order of majesty. The perspective is very much that of a human observer, reading into his or her experience of creation – from the stars in the sky to the fish in the deep – something of the greatness of God.

However, Psalm 8 and other responses to the ordered creation story of Genesis 1—2 sometimes seem inadequate to describe the fractured relationship between the environment, humanity and God. Are there ways to understand that relationship that take seriously the notion that humanity 'made in the image of God' (Genesis 1.26) is also capable of spoiling and misusing God's creation?

The word-picture offered by the last book of the Bible, Revelation, suggests that creation is not a finished product, and awaits the establishment of an even closer relationship between God and humanity. Read Revelation 21.1—6 and 22.1—5, and pick out the themes shared and developed from Genesis 1—3. Note that it is not a case of a perfect spiritual creation replacing a corrupted material universe, but rather of something completely new, made up of familiar elements: trees, rivers, cities and streets. The presence of God, dwelling in the midst of all, will define what it means to exist here. Some have read this vision as referring to life after death; others have read it as an idealised response to the persecution the early Christians were enduring at the hands of the state. It is so centred on the work of God that it runs the risk of encouraging a fatalistic response to the difficulties and injustices of the current creation.

However, it points in the most rich and vivid terms to the role of Jesus Christ in a Christian understanding of creation. Hebrews 1.1—4 describes Christ's creating, sustaining place in the world, and in Hebrews 2.5—9 we find Psalm 8 quoted again, referring to his self-emptying choice to become part of his creation, and to die for it. Creation, incarnation and salvation are all drawn together in the breadth of the Biblical narrative.

Take time to read the texts referred to here, and to compare the ways they understand God as Creator. Are there common and coherent threads, or many different pictures?

Where does everything come from?

The short answer to this question is simply 'God'. This is affirmed by the opening statement of the Apostles' Creed: 'I believe in God, the Father Almighty, maker of heaven and earth.' But the Bible is not alone in affirming that God created the world. Almost all religions have their creation stories, and the philosophers of classical antiquity, especially Plato and Aristotle, assumed that the order and movement of the world must be accounted for by the action of God. To this extent, the idea of creation is a universal theme in religion and philosophy.

But the Bible does not merely repeat what we find elsewhere. The depiction of creation in Scripture is full of distinctive themes of Hebrew and early Christian thought. For this reason, we should not consider Christian teaching about creation only as an account of how the world originated, although that is of course included. The language of creation also attests God's character and purposes, the wisdom and beauty of the world, the value of embodied life, the story of God's covenant partnership with Israel and the nations, and the cosmic significance of Jesus.

Creation in the Bible

The opening two chapters of Genesis offer two different stories of the event of creation, though they also overlap in important respects. These two narratives reflect the dependence of the entire created order upon God – stars and planets, sea and rivers, earth and sky, vegetation and animals. But the first story (Genesis 1.1–2.4a) has a more cosmic scope, while the second story (Genesis 2.4b–3.24) is concentrated on the first human couple, Adam and Eve.

Genesis 1 famously recounts the story of creation in six days. Apart from the Christmas story, it may be the best-known passage in the Bible. The genre is that of proclamation and confession rather than that of a human attempt to explain the existence of the world. Its primary function should be understood as an expression of praise and confession in God. God's good creation is a source of praise. The creation of the world proceeds majestically by a series of commands – the motif of a struggle between God and another power, as is found in other ancient near eastern stories, is absent here. Animals have a central place in this creation story. They precede human beings in the order of creation; later in Genesis the mission of Noah is to save each species from the flood. The first story culminates in the Sabbath rest on the seventh day when the world and its maker rejoice in the harmony and goodness of creation. And the first Sabbath is also the harbinger of a new world when God's good purposes will be finally established.

In the Psalms, there are numerous references to the world as God's good creation even though it is threatened with disruption. Psalms 8, 19 and 104 testify to the beauty and abundance of the natural world, God's providential care for all creatures, and the regulation of human conduct by divine law. There is a clear linkage between natural order, social justice and the worship of God, all of which characterise a harmonious world (Hosea 4.1–3). The language of wisdom in the Old Testament, for example in Proverbs and Job, connects the act of creation with the regulation of natural, social and religious life.

The Jewish concept of wisdom became fused in later thought with the Greek notion of *logos* (the Word). This enables the New Testament writers to connect creation with the person and work of Jesus. The wisdom or Word through which the world is created now becomes a human being, Jesus Christ (John 1.14). By describing creation as Christ-centred, the New Testament unites into a single comprehensive narrative the story of creation and redemption (1 Corinthians 8.6; Colossians 1.15; and Hebrews 1.1–4).

God's good creation
is a source of praise.

Creation in Christian thought

Creation, as we have noted, is not merely about how the universe came about. The description of the world as God's handiwork tells us something of God's nature and purpose. Creation designates the world as other than God but constantly dependent upon God's wise provision. The goodness of the material world is also affirmed, against all those religious tendencies that view matter as seductive and evil.

Yet while creation is in itself good, Scripture teaches that it has not yet reached its appointed end. The order of the world is marred by disruptive forces. The existence of horrendous suffering and evil poses real difficulties to Christian claims about the goodness of creation and its Creator. For this reason also, we should view creation as only the first of God's works – its culmination requires the coming of Jesus into the world. His resurrection from the dead is a decisive sign of the new creation that God intends.

This account of the meaning of Genesis 1 should also allay concerns about a possible conflict with science. We should not read the six days of creation in such a way as to establish a competition with scientific accounts of the beginnings of the universe. A better strategy is to view Genesis 1 as describing in poetic language *why* the world was created, the dependence of everything upon God, and the purpose of human existence. By contrast, modern science deals with *how* questions about natural forces, the emergence of atoms and molecules, the formation of stars and planets, and the evolution of life-forms.

There may be a valuable conversation between science and theology, but we should regard Scripture and contemporary science as dealing with separate questions. Their answers are complementary, not competitive. Faith and science offer very different types of explanation.

> ❝ while creation is in itself good, Scripture teaches that it has not yet reached its appointed end.

Creation 'out of nothing'

Notwithstanding this last point, there are some theoretical elements that are incorporated in the classical Christian understanding of creation. From about the end of the second century, Christian theologians were unanimous in their acceptance of the idea that creation was 'out of nothing' (*creatio ex nihilo*) rather than being out of some pre-existing matter. The Bible does not explicitly affirm this, although some passages point in its direction (Genesis 1.1–2; Romans 4.17; Hebrews 11.3). But there is some ambivalence in the text of Genesis 1.1–2 which is reflected in the variant translations offered in the New Revised Standard Version. The phrases 'a formless void' and 'the face of the deep' appeared to some early thinkers to be consistent with the idea of creation from pre-existent matter. But early theologians such as Irenaeus and Tertullian insisted upon creation 'out of nothing' since this view seemed to be more fitting of the God of the Bible.

This insistence on creation out of nothing directly opposed the two main rival theories in the ancient world – the view that matter itself was eternal (and thus did not need creating), and the view that created things issue forth or emanate from the divine being itself. The first view was the default setting of much ancient philosophy. Here the world was considered to be everlasting, and the work of God was to impose order and regular movement upon a chaotic matter – this position was expressed for example in Plato's famous work *Timaeus*. Even more difficult for Christian theologians was the second view. Here, matter was considered to be inherently imperfect, and to have come about by way of a series of impersonal issues or emanations from the being of the Creator. Both these ideas appeared to strike at Biblical assumptions about divine sovereignty and transcendence, as well as at convictions about the goodness of the world.

To contest these ideas, theologians developed more explicitly the idea that creation was out of nothing rather than from pre-existent matter or out of the divine being itself. To speak of the world being made from nothing broadly indicates that the world is not created from something else (e.g. matter or God). Instead, it proceeds from a free and gracious decision of God.

In structuring the understanding of creation in this way, the Church could relate the power and love of God on one side, to the goodness and otherness of the created world on the other. A framework was thus established for describing the God–world relationship, and subsequent ideas could be placed within this framework. This teaching of creation out of nothing has remained the standard position of Christian theology since the late second century. However, contemporary scholars are anxious to avoid any suggestion that belief in creation out of nothing means that creation is either a random act of God without any purpose or a brute expression of raw divine power. This has been a particular anxiety among feminist writers who are concerned about relationships governed by sheer force. Rather than reflecting an arbitrary and almighty divine will, then, the making of the world out of nothing should be regarded as a reflection of the glory and love of God, as an expression of God's grace and purpose.

Creation and the existence of God

A further development in the Christian understanding of creation was that it came to be associated with a particular type of rational argument for the existence of God called the cosmological argument. Cosmological arguments contend that the only complete explanation for the existing universe is its creation out of nothing by a self-sufficient God. This type of argument has been used by philosophers and theologians in both the Middle Ages and the modern era both to anchor the concept of God in terms of being the One upon whom everything else must be dependent and to reject the views of sceptics who question the very existence of God.

Critics of the cosmological argument, especially at the time of the Enlightenment, have claimed that it is simply not valid, since the world may just exist as a brute fact and may not have any complete explanation. Although this criticism cannot be entirely dispelled, we might say that theology can offer one powerful answer to the unavoidable question 'why is there something rather than nothing?' This answer may fall short of proof and in the end become a matter of faith rather than reason alone. But it does point to the way in which the very existence of our world raises fundamental religious questions.

What does it mean to be a creature?

The opening chapters of the Bible, together with the Psalms and myriad other passages, attest God as Creator. This view entails that everything other than God must have the character of being created. Several related notions are embedded in this relationship of creature to Creator: as dependent, we rely upon God in every moment of our existence; as loved by God, we can flourish and reflect the divine wisdom in our ways of living; as intended by God, each one of us can serve a purpose and, with God's help, we can fulfil our vocation. The creaturely character of our lives is expressed by Scripture in terms of a covenant partnership between God and the world. In entering into such a partnership, God is committed to

- the life of the world (the promise to Noah after the flood)
- the care of Israel as a blessing to the nations (the promise to Abraham and his descendants)
- the Church as a witness to the coming Kingdom of God (the resurrection of Jesus as a sign of the new creation).

The image of God

Much of the discussion about what makes human creatures distinctive from other creatures has revolved around the Biblical notion that we are created in the image and likeness of God (Genesis 1.26–27). Historically, the image of God has often been interpreted as referring to a particular spiritual property or substance that belongs exclusively to human beings (and perhaps also to angels). This has often been identified with the rational mind or soul which human beings possess. Here the influence of the philosophy of Plato has been important, because it identifies the body and the soul as the two components of the human being, and tends to identify the essence of what it means to be human with the non-material soul rather than with the material body. This account of the image of God accords with our intuition that somehow we have a self-conscious awareness and transcendence of our material condition that animals cannot share.

However, this particular account is fraught with problems. The Hebrew Bible does not have nouns that correspond to the Greek words for 'body' and 'soul'. Instead, its anthropology tends to be much more psychosomatic, meaning that it refers to the whole person considered as a coherent unit rather than viewing the human being in terms of different components such as body and soul. Moreover, the restriction of the image of God to some distinctively rational feature of human existence has sometimes led to some groups of people being judged to be less than fully human or as holding the image only in a diminished way – for example, women, different racial groups, or those with learning difficulties. Alongside this, modern biological science has tended to underline the many continuities and similarities between humans and other animals.

We might do better, then, to construct the divine image in terms of a set of functions or relational responsibilities that human beings are given. In this view, the human being is considered to be God's counterpart or representative in creation. Humans are appointed to listen and respond to God, and to represent God's gracious rule on earth. We do this in diverse ways. It requires that we attend to the full range of human activities described in Scripture as reflecting God's wisdom in our households and societies as we learn to exercise responsibility towards other people, other creatures and the wider world. Human beings thus live according to the divine image both by faithfully responding to the world, to one another and to God, and by graciously accepting our dependence on all of these.

> 66 **God is committed to the life of the world**

Human beings, other creatures and the creation

One further problem that arises in this context concerns other creatures. At times in the history of Christian theology, there has been a tendency to see human beings apart from the wider world, as if human beings were the only creatures of intrinsic worth. This has been compounded by interpretations of the command to let human beings 'have dominion' over all the other creatures (Genesis 1.26) as if these other creatures were given to us to possess and exploit as we choose. This 'anthropocentrism', in which human beings place themselves at the centre of creation, has been roundly condemned by recent writers alert to our ecological responsibilities and the ethical claims of other creatures. The problematic notion of 'dominion' requires to be interpreted in a more pastoral direction.

Human beings have a responsibility before God to exercise a proper stewardship of the earth and a genuine care of its other creatures. We are not given a licence to exploit or to pillage the earth. Given our culpability in the pollution of land, sea and air, in the extinction of species, and in the conditions in which many animals are bred, kept and slaughtered for human consumption, this responsibility before God should weigh heavily upon us. In our interactions with other creatures and the material world, we can recall the concern of Old Testament injunctions to respect the land and those animals whose habitat we share (for example, Deuteronomy 22.4; Proverbs 12.10). At other times, we may be called upon simply 'to let the world be'. This might involve, for example, not interfering with wilderness areas where animals and plants can flourish and die apart from any human disruption.

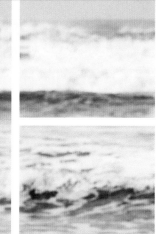

Douglas John Hall, a contemporary Canadian theologian, has stressed that our understanding of the image of God should articulate not only a vertical stress on the special nature of the relationship between God and human beings; it should also include a horizontal emphasis upon relationships between human beings and between human beings and other creatures. Along this second axis, important notions of creaturely interdependence and communion find their rightful place. Hall thus speaks of life in three dimensions – with God, with our neighbours and with the natural world. These are the 'counterparts of our human being', and we cannot live well in one dimension without doing so in the others.[1] For the Bible, all three sets of relation are bound together so that we can only love and serve God, if we also love and serve the earth and our fellow creatures. This multi-dimensional perspective is needed to understand our particularity as human beings and our affinity with the natural world and other animals.

1. Douglas John Hall, *Imaging God: Dominion as Stewardship* (Grand Rapids: Eerdmans, 1987), p. 68.

QUESTIONS

1. What are the different themes of the two creation stories at the opening of Genesis?

2. Why do so many people assume that there is a conflict between science and faith?

3. How might we think of human beings as distinctive without detriment to our view of the wider world and our companion creatures?

darkness, light
good, bad
better, best
sunshine, shadow
endings, beginnings
question, answer
faith, doubt
words, silence
Creator God,
there is so much choice,
so many shades of meaning,
so many angles to explore,
so many refinements to make,
so many answers to unanswerable questions.
Be with those who explore the Universe
that their scientific endeavour
may enrich humanity.
Be with those who listen attentively
to the planets, to other people, to Your Spirit
that in the depths love may be seen and heard.
Be with those engaged in learning
that they may be touched with awe and wonder
as You unfold the secrets of Your Creation.
Lord of time and space,
You are within us and around us,
beyond us and apart from us,
open us up
to the mysteries of Your grace
seen and heard in the person of Jesus,
firstborn of creation and of the dead,
to whom be all glory and praise,
now and for aye.

GOD THE SAVIOUR

Bible Study: Alison Jack

Reflection: Paul T. Nimmo

Prayer: David D. Scott

BIBLE STUDY

'In Christ God was reconciling the world to himself'
2 Corinthians 5.19

Philippians 2.5–11
2 Corinthians 5.16–21
John 10.10

The apostle Paul wrote his letters some time before the Gospel accounts of Jesus' life, death and resurrection were completed, but he has a very clear idea of who Jesus was and is. In Philippians 2.5–11, he offers a description of Jesus' status before he came to earth and the meaning of his life as it was lived here. Paul goes on to describe the consequence of Jesus' obedient living and dying in cosmic terms. This section of Paul's letter is sometimes considered to be a poem or hymn which was used in the early Church, and which Paul is simply quoting. It repays very careful reading, in several different versions of the Bible if you have them, as the language is condensed and there are various ways to translate what is said here.

Of course it is important to remember that this hymn was written for a particular situation in the church at Philippi, to which situation Paul was responding. But it may also help us to articulate an understanding of the person of Jesus Christ, in the early Church and for ourselves. In the passage, Jesus has a privileged status with God from the very beginning. He chooses to give this up to become a person who submits himself to the death of a common criminal. As a result, God exalts him to a position of equality with God which will lead to him being worshipped by all.

In the passage, the subject changes in verse 9 from Jesus Christ to God: there is a distinction made between the two. In other letters, Paul reflects more on this relationship between Jesus and God: a good example is at 2 Corinthians 5.16–21. Here, as verse 19 notes, 'In Christ God was reconciling the world to himself'. God is clearly understood to be acting 'in Christ' in the work of salvation. Compare this passage with Philippians 2.5–11, noting the similarities and differences in understanding who Christ was and is, and what he did.

In both passages, the theological reflections about the person, nature and work of Christ are offered for a purpose: to encourage believers to imitate Christ in their self-understanding and in their actions. Theology and action are brought together. The Gospel of John comes from a very different time and place from Paul and his letters, but there are many similarities in the way he presents Jesus' ministry. According to John, Jesus explains that he has come so that his followers 'may have life, and have it abundantly' (John 10.10). That seems an appealing and suggestive way to articulate a difficult theological concept. Are there other ways to express or define the person and work of Jesus Christ?

Who is Jesus Christ?

The person of Jesus Christ stands at the centre of the Christian faith. And just as he asked the first disciples, so too he asks people today: 'who do you say that I am?' (Matthew 16.15).

In the present as well as in the past, people have answered that question in very different ways. But at a minimal level, most people today, including non-Christians, would accept that Jesus of Nazareth was a real person – someone who lived as a carpenter in Galilee in the first century, before he became a religious teacher and prophet, and ultimately met his demise on a cross one Passover in Jerusalem.

Our key source for knowing about Jesus is the Bible, and in particular the four Gospels. These texts were written by early believing Christians, and are thus in one sense documents of faith: their primary purpose is not to provide a neutral account of history. Instead, to draw on Luke's words, it was 'to write an orderly account ... so that you may know the truth concerning the things about which you have been instructed' (Luke 1.3–4). However, the Gospels are nevertheless full of historical detail, portraying real people and real places, and have their roots in the accounts and experiences of early followers who actually knew Jesus.

The historical person of Jesus that the Gospels describe is in many ways a very human figure. Jesus is not an alien spirit or a fantastic illusion, as some have wanted to claim at different points in history, but a genuinely human being. He is a person who talks, who eats, who cries, who sleeps, who prays, who ultimately dies. Jesus knows what it is to celebrate and to rejoice, and he also knows what it is to be tempted, to be disappointed, even to be betrayed. Whatever else Jesus may be, then, as early Christians recognised, he is never less than truly human – indeed, we are told, he became 'like his brothers and sisters in every respect' (Hebrews 2.17).

For all that Jesus was human like the rest of us, however, the early disciples came to believe that there was also something wonderfully, challengingly different about Jesus – a more-than-human quality to his person. Their encounter with Jesus led them to leave behind their jobs, their families and their possessions in order to follow him. They observed that Jesus claimed a special relationship with God, teaching about God with authority and performing signs and wonders in the name of God. And not only that: he was happy to oppose the scribes and Pharisees and the prevailing religious wisdom of the day; he spent time with those who were lowly and outcast, visiting their houses, dining with them, and proclaiming the forgiveness of sins; and he rightly predicted his own suffering and crucifixion. When the mission of

early Christians came to believe that Jesus was the pivotal point of God's eternal plan of salvation.

Jesus seemed to end in failure on the cross, his followers declared that Jesus had been raised from the dead, and that he spent time among them on earth before being taken up into heaven.

In their reflections on this last, stunning turn of events, early Christians came to believe that Jesus was the pivotal point of God's eternal plan of salvation. This plan began with God's creation of all things out of nothing, ran through the history of God's covenant with Israel, and reached its climax in the incarnation of God in Jesus. It was out of this central event – through the life, ministry, crucifixion, resurrection and ascension of Jesus as Immanuel, God with us – that there came the sending of the Spirit at Pentecost, and the subsequent gathering in and sending out of the Church. Yet even this was not the end of the divine intention for us: God's plan was prophesied to find its ultimate fulfilment in the return of Jesus at the end of time, in the full unveiling of the Kingdom of God against the backdrop of a new heaven and a new earth.

The kind of language used to describe Jesus in Scripture – 'Son of God', 'Word', 'Messiah', 'Saviour' – reflects early Christian attempts to do justice to this

special dimension of the life of Jesus. One of the most stirring confessions of this early Christian faith is that of Thomas the doubting disciple when he came face to face with the risen Jesus: 'My Lord and my God' (John 20.28).

But the lack of precision in such language also led to a long and difficult series of debates in the early Church. The initial difficulty arose because Christians, like Jews, confessed one God as Father, so that there could be no talk for either group of there being two gods. Yet Christians also confessed Jesus Christ as Lord and Saviour, which implied that Jesus was somehow divine and thus somehow related to God. This tension, and different ways of understanding what it means to call Jesus 'Word of God', famously led the Roman Emperor Constantine to call a Church council at Nicaea in 325, which issued a confession of faith intended to resolve the matter.

This document – as revised in 381 – can be found in our hymn-books under the title 'The Nicene Creed'. Its text states as part of its confession of faith that Jesus Christ is 'God from God, Light from Light, true God from true God'. What this means is that, for the Church, Jesus is not a lesser God than God the Father but is of the same being or essence as God the Father and is thus also truly God. And this is a truly radical confession: Jesus is not only truly human, but also truly God.

This description of Jesus Christ, as both fully divine and fully human, has been the consensus position of most Christians since the days of the early Church, and remains the official position of the majority of Christian churches today. But it is a confession that has not been without its share of controversy. This view has been criticised, not only outwith but also within the Church, particularly in more recent times, by those who interpret the way in which Scripture speaks of Jesus differently and who in turn deny the claim of Nicaea. Even among church-goers, it is not uncommon to find Jesus thought of simply as a human being – perhaps as an exceptional human being, as a divinely inspired teacher, but not as the Son of God. In this view, there is no mystery of the incarnation, and the Word has not become flesh and dwelt among us (cf. John 1.14).

For other Christians, however, belief that Jesus is the Son of God is grounded not only in the words of Scripture and in the tradition of the Church, but also in the experience they have of relationship with Jesus in the present day. In prayer and in worship, in sermon and in sacrament, many Christians come to know the presence of Jesus and to hear the voice of Jesus, and to confess him as truly divine.

This sense of encounter is not only alive in the course of events and activities in the Church. Christians believe that Jesus draws near to them in the everyday and the routine – while making dinner, while reading quietly, while working steadily, while sitting peacefully. In each case, Christians believe, the One who comes to meet us, to comfort us and to challenge us is the One who was born to us, who walked among us, who died for us and who rose again. Though times change, and everything around us changes, still it is the case that this Jesus Christ is the same, a constant presence – comforting and challenging, yesterday, today and for ever (Hebrews 13.8).

What does Jesus Christ do for us?

One of the confessions of the earliest Christians was 'Jesus Christ, Son of God, Saviour'. If the first letter of each word of this is written down in Greek, the Greek word 'fish' is spelled out – perhaps one reason why the fish was used as an early Christian symbol. But to call Jesus 'Saviour' in this way has two immediate implications: first, it suggests that there is something from which people need to be saved; and second, it suggests that Jesus is the One who performs this saving activity. Both of these suggestions require a little further unpacking.

First, what is the threat from which we need to be saved? In Scripture, this threat is described using many different terms. In some texts, the enemy that is in view is said to be death, or the corruption of the body. In other texts, the enemy that is in view is said to be the devil, or the power of darkness. Perhaps most commonly, the enemy that is in view is spoken of as sin.

For all this variety, there is no sense in Scripture that these threats are different or unrelated. Instead, they are all seen to be part of the same complex of evil that has haunted creation since the earliest days of humanity, the same complex of evil that opposed the life and ministry of Jesus Christ and that – though overcome by Jesus Christ – continues yet to afflict the world in the present day. And what this variety of terms seems to suggest is that this evil has a power and a depth that impacts not only upon every aspect of human life but also upon every aspect of creation. It is the testimony of Scripture at every point that, in face of such an opponent, human beings have no power to save themselves. By contrast, they are utterly reliant for their salvation upon God.

Second, then, what is it that Jesus Christ does to save human beings from this enemy? In trying to describe the salvation that Jesus accomplishes in all its fullness, Scripture draws on a series of images from different spheres of life. And so we find in Scripture financial images from the world of the slave-market ('redemption' and 'ransom'), military images of victory (over the 'power of darkness'), sacrificial images from the world of the Jewish temple ('blood of the covenant' and 'sacrifice of atonement') and legal images from the world of the law-court ('condemnation' and 'justification'). All of these images are used in order to attempt to shed light on the reality of salvation and what it means. And again – just as with the different terms used to describe the full scope and depth of sin – there is no sense of competition or conflict between them. Indeed, in many texts in Scripture, an author uses different images within the same verse.

As later Christians reflected further on the event of salvation with the help of these various images, they developed a number of different patterns of thinking about the work of Jesus, each offering its own particular insights and emphases.

Four different patterns of thinking about the work of salvation might be mentioned:

- One pattern of thinking about salvation emphasises the fact of the incarnation itself, highlighting that the Word becoming flesh in Jesus Christ is an event that is transformative of human existence. It is in the very act of becoming human that the Word overcomes the death and corruption that afflicts us, and restores us to our originally intended goodness. Thus it is precisely the union of the divine and the human in Jesus Christ that brings about our salvation.

- Another pattern of thinking focuses on the ministry of Jesus and the example of human living that he sets before us. In the substance of his teaching, in the compassion of his actions, and in the openness of his relationships, there is seen on earth the image of God in human form that we are called to emulate. As Christians, we are inspired and empowered by this perfect example to respond with a new love not only for God but also for our neighbour.

- A third pattern of thinking is centred on the passion and crucifixion of Jesus, emphasising that Jesus takes the place of human sinners in going to the cross. In a miraculous exchange, the sinless Jesus becomes sin, taking on our sins for our sake and suffering the punishment and God-abandonment that we are due. At the same time, and as a result, we no longer have our sins counted against us, but are considered by God to be righteous in Christ.

- A further pattern of thinking highlights the way in which Jesus is sent into the world by God to oppose and defeat the powers of darkness that are oppressing the creation and its creatures. In this vision there is a spiritual battle encompassing the whole of creation, and Jesus represents the radically new intervention of God in history. In Jesus, God invades the old creation ruled by sin, delivering it from the forces of evil, and establishing the new creation.

These different patterns all have their roots in the witness of Scripture, even as they are not always easy to harmonise in their details. Different patterns have proven attractive to different churches and different Christians at different times as they have reflected upon our salvation in Christ. In the tradition of the Church of Scotland in particular, and of the Protestant tradition more generally, the third pattern of thinking has had most influence, though not to the exclusion of the other patterns outlined.

What is common to all of these ways of thinking about salvation is that they all depend on the event of the resurrection. As the apostle Paul writes, 'if Christ has not been raised, then our proclamation has been in vain and your faith has been in vain' (1 Corinthians 15.14). Without the resurrection, the salvation accomplished in Jesus Christ would not be known, and the new life and new creation inaugurated by him would not be accomplished. For all the scepticism concerning whether the resurrection actually happened – a scepticism that was as vigorous at the time of the disciples as it is in our own time – this event thus stands at the very inception of the Christian faith.

How, then, might we try to articulate what salvation means for Christians today?

We might try and capture the essence of the work of Jesus in salvation by stating that what Jesus

does is to restore us to right relationship with God. In the language of the Christian tradition, Jesus makes us 'at one' with God, and thus achieves the work of 'at-one-ment', or atonement.

What this means is that, despite our manifold errors and evident shortcomings, Jesus encounters us today with the assurance that he has overcome and forgiven all our failures, and that we can come before God without fear and call upon God as Father. To speak of Jesus as the Saviour, therefore, is to indicate on the one hand our liberation from the powers of oppression that afflict us – from the regrets, frustrations and mistakes that haunt us and from the abiding and pervading sense of brokenness that accompanies us in this world. And it is to indicate on the other hand our calling and empowerment to become and to be the good creatures of God that we were purposed to be – living in harmony with God, with each other, with our world, with ourselves.

" in the work of Jesus Christ, the dawn of salvation has truly come

To speak of the work of Jesus Christ in this way suggests that being or becoming a Christian is no small matter. Indeed, the apostle Paul writes that 'if anyone is in Christ, there is a new creation' (2 Corinthians 5.17). The effect of the work of Jesus Christ is that we gain nothing less than a new sense of identity, a new perspective on life, and a new orientation of purpose. Certainly, the full reality of salvation has not yet been revealed either in the world or in our lives – there is still evil in the world, and we are still its agents and its victims, caught between our new life in Christ and our old existence under sin. In this sense, the work of Jesus Christ is not yet complete, and we are in need of the ongoing liberation and empowerment of God.

Christians confess, however, that in the person and in the work of Jesus Christ, the dawn of salvation has truly come and the Kingdom of God has truly been inaugurated on earth. He is the 'one Mediator between God and humanity' (1 Timothy 2.5) – the One who as truly human and truly divine reconciles us with God, and who reconciles us with God as the One who is truly human and truly divine. Who he is and what he does are thus ultimately different sides of the same, saving reality – the one Jesus Christ who Christians believe to be Saviour and Lord of all.

QUESTIONS

1. Why might the early Church have considered it so important to confess that Jesus Christ is both fully divine and fully human?

2. What does 'salvation' mean to you – what do you feel that you are saved from, and what do you feel that you are being saved for?

3. What would be some ways of sharing the Christian belief in salvation with those who do not know much about the Christian faith?

Lord,
You have borne our suffering
like a king
with a crown of thorns upon Your head.
You have ministered to Your people
like a servant
humbly washing feet.
You have revealed Your grace
like a sinner
embracing unclean people with integrity and joy.
You have proclaimed Your gospel
like a fool
dying on a cross with forgiveness on Your lips.
Perhaps for a good person
someone might actually dare to die?
But You prove Your love for us
in that while we were yet sinners,
Christ died for us.
Forgive us our sins.
Purify our hearts.
Inspire us to minister Your grace.
You have said, 'Ask!'
and we ask for mercy.
You have said, 'Seek!'
and we search for peace.
You have said, 'Knock!'
and we open the door
to a King in servant's clothing,
waiting at table to break bread and share wine
and lead us to a cross and a crown
and a life lived for others
in the love which is eternal.

GOD THE SPIRIT

Bible Study: Alison Jack

Reflection: Sarah Lane Ritchie

Prayer: David D. Scott

BIBLE STUDY

'I will pour out my Spirit upon all flesh'

Joel 2.28

Ezekiel 37.1–14
Acts 2.1–21
Joel 2.28–32
Acts 1.4–5, 8

The English words 'spirit', 'wind' and 'breath' have all been used as translations of one Hebrew word, *ruach*, and one Greek word, *pneuma*. These breathy words are all applied to the person of the Trinity known as the Holy Spirit. While this aspect of the being of God is hard to pin down, perhaps two stories in which spirit appears will help us to understand the Spirit better.

The first is Ezekiel 37.1–14, which begins with a great expanse of dry bones. Read the story and carefully consider the role that breath/spirit plays at each stage. What is the nature of the life that is described and promised to the hearers and that the Spirit brings?

Prophecy and the work of the Spirit are closely linked in the Old Testament, and this extends into the New Testament. Our second story comes from the Day of Pentecost, when the Spirit enables people from all corners of the world to hear 'the great things God has done'. Read Acts 2.1–21, and compare the role of the Spirit here with the role of the Spirit in the Ezekiel passage. This is new life available to all, anchored in the prophecies of the past (Joel 2.28–32), and it is the outcome of the promise made by Jesus at the ascension (see Acts 1.4–5, 8).

Fire and wind are the images used in the Acts story to describe the effect of the Spirit on those who were in the right place at the right time to feel its power. Explosive and unpredictable, the Spirit swept up those who had gathered where Jesus had told them to be. They were together and they were waiting, ready to share the good news. They had to be prepared and willing to become the prophets Jesus needed them to be – whether they were men or women, the old or the young, the slave or the free.

In the light of the story of Pentecost, consider ways in which you and today's Church are in the right place at the right time for the Spirit to come and make its presence felt. Whose are the voices that represent the surprisingly diverse range of participants detailed in Joel 2.28–32 and Acts 2.17–21, and are these voices being heard and valued today?

Who is the Spirit?

Wrapping our minds around the person and work of the Spirit is probably one of the most perplexing and challenging aspects of the Christian faith. When we think about the Trinity – the three-in-one relationship of Father, Son and Spirit – we often begin with the Father. The Father is the Creator, Source and Sustainer of all existence: while certainly beyond our mental grasp, there is something about God as Father and Creator that we can conceptualise. Then we come to the Son, Jesus Christ. Jesus was a real person – fully God, but also a real human being. Again, while the incarnation is endlessly perplexing, there is something concrete and even *earthy* about Jesus. But then we get to the Spirit, and our minds come up empty: how exactly can we think about the Spirit, an immaterial reality who escapes concrete language – and yet is fully God?

While the Spirit may be inherently mysterious for us as finite humans, we can at least gain some understanding by identifying who the Spirit is in relation to God and the Trinity. Put simply, the Spirit *is* God – just as the Father and the Son are fully God, so is the Spirit. This is an important point, and one that is often minimised. After all, we live in a time when all things 'spiritual' are sometimes viewed with immense scepticism. Western sensibilities are often more comfortable with empirical, tangible realities, and we are taught to be wary of antiquated ways of thinking and talking about 'spirits'. It can be easy to think of the Spirit as *a* spirit of the Father or Jesus, much as we might say that someone was 'with us in spirit', or that a friend has 'a lively spirit'.

But this way of talking about 'spirit' has little to do with *the* Spirit. To speak of the Spirit is thus not to use shorthand in referring to the Father's presence or the Son's activity among us. No, the Spirit is a full member of the Trinity and as much God as are the Father and the Son. As such, we worship the Spirit just as we worship the Father and the Son.

And yet, it remains difficult for us to grasp completely the reality of the Spirit as a fully fledged member of the Trinity precisely because the Spirit does not always seem to be *personal* to us. We think of God the Father not only as Creator but also as *Father*, together with all the personal qualities that come along with such a parental role. Jesus, on the other hand, was a real person who spoke audible words and lived a human life; there is something relatable and personal about Jesus.

But the Spirit is more difficult, and it is important to acknowledge this. The Bible often speaks about 'spirit' in ways that do not seem personal, using words like 'breath' or 'wind'. For example, the same Hebrew word (*ruach*) that is sometimes translated as 'wind' (Genesis 1.2) in the story of creation is the same word used by Moses to describe the Spirit of God (Numbers 11.29). Moreover, it is not always clear when the Bible is talking about creaturely 'spirits' or *the Spirit*. Frankly, understanding God the Spirit can be confusing, precisely because the Spirit does not fit into tidy, comfortable categories. It took Christians centuries of deliberation to come to an understanding of the Trinity that included the full personhood of the Spirit, distinct from but intertwined with the persons of the Father and of the Son.

How, then, did early Christians come to affirm that the Spirit is God? It is rather a complicated story, but we can see that early Christians drew not only upon the written Scripture, but also upon the lived experience of actual Christians. The Bible itself speaks in a great variety of ways about the Spirit. The Old Testament speaks of 'the Spirit of God', using various words that mean 'breath' or 'wind'. The Spirit is often linked to God's creative activity, both at the moment of creation (Genesis 1 and 2.7) and throughout history (for example, Ezekiel 37.5–6). This is key to understanding the Spirit and its work: the Spirit is vital to the bringing forth and sustaining of all life. At the same time, the Spirit is seen as drawing individuals and communities into a fuller understanding of God's purposes for the world. Indeed, the Spirit of God empowers the nation of Israel to act justly and mercifully and to 'bring good news to the oppressed' (Isaiah 61.1), and restores hope to Israel when all hope seemed lost.

In the New Testament, we see the Spirit discussed much more prominently and definitively. The Spirit is vital to the life and ministry of Jesus. Jesus was 'full of the Holy Spirit' (Luke 4.1) and 'rejoiced in the Holy Spirit' (Luke 10.21). Indeed, Jesus speaks of 'the Spirit of truth' (John 14.17), and of the Spirit as the One from whom believers receive comfort and instruction (John 14.26). Importantly, Jesus speaks of the Spirit as being intimately connected not only with himself, but with God the Father. We see in the New Testament strong hints of what would become known as the Trinity: the unity and inter-relationships of Father, Son and Spirit. Also in the New Testament, we see early Christians encountering the Spirit on the day of Pentecost, after Jesus had risen from the dead and ascended to the Father. On that day, Jesus' followers were 'filled with the Holy Spirit' (Acts 2.4). The Spirit came to fill believers with the presence and love of God, but not independently: rather, the Spirit was sent from the Father and through the Son.

As the early Church struggled to put into words the relationships between Father, Son and Spirit, they wrestled with Scripture texts in light of their lived experience of faith and came to confess the full divinity of the Spirit. But what does it mean for the Spirit to be fully divine?

Christians have often emphasised the vital importance of the *relational* nature

the Spirit is vital to the bringing forth and sustaining of all life.

of the Trinity. Yes, Father, Son and Spirit are distinct persons – but they exist only in intimate relationship with each other. They are not separate beings, but exist only in a loving and dynamic communion. Indeed, the Spirit has often been thought of as the energy and love that binds the Trinity. The Spirit has also been thought of as the creative presence of God in creation. And yet, the Spirit never acts alone, but always in unity with the Son and the Father. The energetic love of the Spirit in relation to the Father and the Son is reflected and manifested in the Spirit's activity in the world. Indeed, 'God has sent the Spirit of his Son into our hearts' (Galatians 4.6) – there is a direct relationship between who the Spirit is in relationship to the Father and Son, and who the Spirit is for humanity.

In trying to understand the Spirit, we will always come up against the limits of language and our finite capacity to understand. There is certainly something mysterious about God the Spirit! It is not surprising that the person and role of the Spirit has long been debated in Christian history. And yet, the impossibility of containing the Spirit in a neat, tidy box is not merely a conceptual *problem* – it is an exciting possibility. If the Spirit refuses to be defined and conceptualised, then this prevents us from objectifying God and attempting to control or limit God's activity. There is something untamed and surprising about God's active presence, and this is never more clear than when we speak of the Spirit.

What does the Spirit do for us?

In affirming the Spirit as fully God, we recognise that the personhood of the Spirit entails a certain uniqueness in the Spirit's role and activity. God the Father is the Creator and Sustainer of all life, and God the Son is the Redeemer of all creation. But what does the Spirit actually do, not only for us, but also for the wider creation?

First, it is impossible to separate the Spirit's work from the life, death and resurrection of Jesus Christ. God the Spirit works *in* us, enabling us to participate in the reconciliation between God and humanity that Jesus achieved. The apostle Paul wrote that 'you were washed, you were sanctified, you were justified in the name of the Lord Jesus Christ and in the Spirit of our God' (1 Corinthians 6.11). Jesus lived over 2,000 years ago – we in the present century are far removed from his teachings, miracles and revelation. But the Spirit makes Christ present to us, bridging the temporal and historical gap between us and Jesus. Because of the Spirit, Christ's words and saving power are not merely historical accounts or distant memories – no, they are made real to us now through the Spirit.

In fact, Jesus and the Spirit are interdependent: Jesus both received and was empowered by the Spirit, even as he also gave the Spirit to his followers. Because the Spirit was poured out on Christians at Pentecost and remains with us still, we have immediate access to the transformative truth of Jesus. It is by the Spirit that we are reconciled to God through Christ, liberated from sin and fear, and empowered to grow in the knowledge of God's love and justice. The Spirit has been 'poured out on us richly through Jesus Christ our Saviour, so that, having been justified by his grace, we might become heirs according to the hope of eternal life' (Titus 3.6–7).

As we have seen, there are often understandable challenges in grasping the concept of the Spirit as truly personal; now, however, we see that the Spirit could not be *more* personal. Indeed, it is the Spirit who connects us individually and communally to the work of Christ; it is the Spirit who draws us personally into an experiential knowledge of Jesus and the Father.

Let us unpack this further. One way of exploring the work of the Spirit in our lives is to examine three ways in which the Spirit is active in us: illumination, empowerment and inspiration.

First, illumination: the Spirit draws us to God and *illuminates* our hearts and minds so that they are open to the truth of Jesus Christ. God reveals truth to us 'through the Spirit; for the Spirit searches everything, even the depths of God' (1 Corinthians 2.10). Indeed, without the Spirit, we could have no knowledge of God – let alone be reconciled to God through Christ. Many Christians have used in this connection the term 'prevenient grace' to describe the way in which the Spirit 'goes before us' in our spiritual journeys. Before we are even aware of God's presence or truth, the Spirit is at work in us to draw us to God, and Scripture tells us of Jesus' promise that the Spirit 'will guide you into all the truth' (John 16.13).

The way this happens can be very diverse, depending on individual situations. For example, the Spirit may illuminate our minds to see God at work in a certain person or situation, or to recognise God in the beauty of a piece of music. Alternatively, we may feel guilty or ashamed of the ways we have harmed ourselves or others, acting out of spite, pride or anger. It is the Spirit who makes us aware of our brokenness and need for God, and it is the Spirit who shows us the promise of reconciliation and hope for unity with God and with each other. The Spirit illuminates the reality of God's love in our minds, increasing our desire for transformation and wholeness.

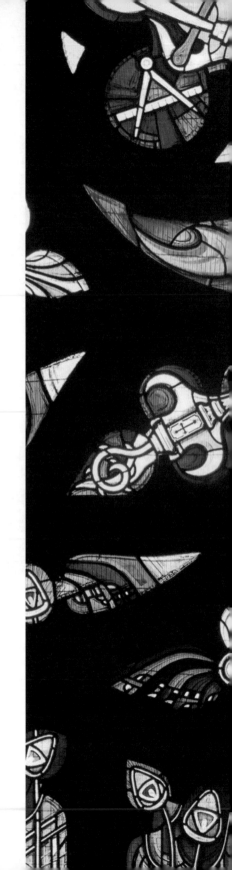

SACRUM · MYSTERIUM

get beyond theoretical abstractions about God, and actually encounter God. Even more than this, 'you are in the Spirit, since the Spirit of God dwells in you' (Romans 8.9). Encountering God in prayer is a transformative process, emboldening and empowering us to live our lives thereafter in ways that demonstrate this transformation. Because the Spirit fills us and enables us to participate in God's presence, we are able to live our lives in a Christ-like way, acting with kindness, grace, truth and justice.

Finally, inspiration: the Spirit *inspires* us. Scripture tells us that 'God's love has been poured into our hearts through the Holy Spirit that has been given to us' (Romans 5.5), and this enables us to see truth, think creatively and act boldly. Through the Spirit, we are inspired to see what love, grace and justice mean in different situations. We are inspired to produce art, music and poetry, or to challenge unjust political structures. The Christian faith is not static; it is not as if God's relationship with creation stopped at the time of Jesus – even now, 'the Spirit gives life' (2 Corinthians 3.6). The saving work of Jesus was indeed the definitive revelation of God to the world, but it is the Spirit who continues to work in and with humans to reveal the truth of Christ and bring healing to a broken world; for 'where the Spirit of the Lord is, there is freedom' (2 Corinthians 3.17). Christians are called to be creative partners with the Spirit in dynamically engaging, in very specific ways, with the world around us.

The Spirit draws us into God's love and grace even before we know that we desire those things!

Second, empowerment: the Spirit not only awakens our hearts to our need for God's salvation and justification, but *empowers* us to grow in the knowledge of God and to follow the teachings of Christ. Jesus told his disciples that they would 'receive power when the Holy Spirit has come upon you' to be witnesses of Christ 'to the ends of the earth' (Acts 1.8–9). Christians often speak of discipleship, of growing in truth, love, mercy and justice. It is the Spirit that empowers us to do these things, even as we remain flawed human beings in need of grace.

One of the ways in which the Spirit empowers us is through prayer. The Bible tells us that 'the Spirit helps us in our weakness; for we do not know how to pray as we ought, but that very Spirit intercedes' (Romans 8.26). The Spirit is kind, loving and dynamic, drawing us deeper into God's presence through prayer. By empowering us to pray, the Spirit makes it possible for us to experience a relationship with God that is real and *felt*. Through the Spirit in prayer, we

Being filled with the Spirit, we are able to engage creatively with culture, politics, education and relationships, exploring ways in which Christian truths might be applied in an ever-changing world. The Spirit inspires us to live freely, openly, even playfully. Our faith is not to be stagnant or boring, but simultaneously engaged with the world and with God. Christians have often talked about the cosmic dimensions of the Spirit – the ways in which the Spirit is active in all of creation, not just the Church. We recognise and partner with the Spirit we see moving in the world: in troubled communities, in political situations and in our families. Because the Spirit is always present and active in the world, we can learn to recognise the Spirit at work around us – Christians often call this process 'discernment'. We can discern the Spirit at work not only through the Bible or worship, but also through the natural sciences, art, history, and even other religions.

It might be tempting to be wary of the Spirit. After all, the Spirit resists definition, containment and control – the Spirit is not tame! It can be unsettling to recognise or affirm the Spirit's activity in or around us when it might draw us outside of our comfort zones. But it is in just these times that Christians can remember and take comfort in knowing that the Spirit is God – the same God who lovingly creates us, and the same God who brings salvation, hope and joy through Jesus. When we live in the Spirit, we are comforted even as we are stretched and challenged – life in the Spirit is an adventure, but one that is full of the assurance of God's love and presence.

QUESTIONS

1. Where do you see the Spirit at work in your life, and how might the Spirit be seeking to lead you out of your comfort zone?

2. Where do you see the Spirit at work in the world, such as in scientific discovery, political situations or cultural movements?

3. The Spirit is notoriously difficult to define or 'pin down' – are you uncomfortable with this level of uncertainty about the Spirit, or do you welcome the 'wildness' of God?

Lord,
the wind blows
and we cannot see it
but we can hear it in the tree
and feel its refreshment on our face –
so it is with Your Spirit!
the fire burns
and we see its vibrant colours
and feel its radiance
enfolding us in its warmth and light –
so it is with Your Spirit!
the dove descends
down to earth
and we see its snow-white wing
and marvel at its grace and gentleness –
so it is with Your Spirit!
Like the wind,
blow away the things which clutter up our lives;
like the fire,
burn up the unworthy things within us;
like the dove,
move us with gentleness and grace.
Forgive us,
refresh us,
heal us
and set us afire with Your love
that we may bring forth
the fruits of Your Spirit –
joy,
love,
peace
through Jesus Christ,
our Saviour and Lord.

THE CHRISTIAN CHURCH

Bible Study: **Alison Jack**

Reflection: **Sandy Forsyth**

Prayer: **David D. Scott**

BIBLE STUDY

'Go, therefore, and make disciples of all nations'
Matthew 28.19

Micah 4.1-5
Matthew 28.16-20
John 12.1-8 and 13.1-15

In Micah 4.1-5 a vision is offered of a mountain which is the house or dwelling place of God, and to which people of all nations come. There they receive teaching from God and guidance about walking in God's paths. Hearing the word of God, and being in the presence of God, leads to peace and stability for individuals and communities.

In Matthew 28.16-20, the risen Christ meets his disciples on a mountain in Galilee. Being in his presence leads some to worship, although some who doubt are also there. Jesus gives them a manifesto, or commission, based on his heavenly and earthly authority. He tells his disciples to go and make disciples of people of all nations, baptising them in the name of the Trinity, and teaching them the way of life he has passed on to them. He promises his presence wherever they go, for all time.

Being in the presence of God, in the company of others; hearing and applying the teaching received; and reaching out to those who have yet to know God, seem to be at the heart of the Biblical understanding of what it means to be a worshipping community.

Many different word-pictures to describe the Church are offered in the New Testament, particularly in the letters of Paul and others to the communities of the early Church. Often these word-pictures are designed to correct a church community which has gone wrong somehow, in the opinion of the writer. But there are two stories in John's Gospel which might help us to understand better what it means to be the Church today. Read John 12.1-8 and 13.1-15. Here are two stories about foot washing. The first is an expression of love, even worship, an acknowledgement of the presence of the divine in the midst of the ordinary. The second is a demonstration of radical service and sacrifice, offered as an example to be lived and followed … and, just as importantly, to be accepted and received.

In what ways does your church respond to Jesus' commission in Matthew 28?

What are the points of connection between your experience of the Church and the stories of foot washing in John's Gospel? How might these points of connection be made stronger?

What is the Church?

As Christians are sent by God to fulfil God's Kingdom goals for the world, so the Church is the gathering of a community of people who understand themselves to be the agents of God's mission. So what is the Church of such people called – in hope, humility and expectation – to be and to do? How do we understand and practise God's core purposes for the Church? These are significant questions for the meaning of the faith of each person, for the task of the Church, and for how we are to express the gospel in conjunction with our brothers and sisters in Christ.

A primary purpose of the Church is to worship and glorify God, and to fulfil God's intentions for our lives, for humanity and for all creation, with Christ as the head and inspiration. The form and content of how we are to do this within a gathered group of believers, guided by the Word of God and the movement of the Spirit, is the challenge of prayer, discernment and revelation that faces us.

In the New Testament, the 'ecclesia', meaning 'assembly' or congregation, marked a distinctive form of new life and community, centred on the worship of God, service to the world and mutual love and support. These core aspects of the Church continue to define much of its existence, as the Church looks to provide a loving home for the growth of personal and community devotion and faith, and serves as a hub for the people of God exercising that faith by participating in God's mission in the world.

There are many images used to depict the 'ecclesia' in the New Testament. Some are familiar, such as 'the salt of the earth' (Matthew 5.13) and 'the bride of Christ' (see Ephesians 5.23–32). Perhaps the most striking image of all is the notion of the Church as 'the body of Christ' (1 Corinthians 12.27): despite our differing appearances and gifts, we are all united for a common goal, and equal in baptism, in faith and in the Spirit, with a mutual need for Christ as the 'true vine' (John 15.1).

Such images and models of the 'ecclesia' in the New Testament also have implications for understanding the purpose of the Church. Each has strong positive implications for our churches today, but each also carries its own dangers. Four of these images might be briefly recounted here.

- The first image is of the Church as the people of God (1 Peter 2.9). In this view, the Church exists in continuity with the covenant people of Israel. The Church is not an institution or a building, so much as a missional, 'tent' community. This idea has led to the Church being described as a 'sacrament of salvation' to the world. The danger of such a model, however, is that it might risk a Church that exhibits a sense of triumphal self-satisfaction, considering itself to be fully redeemed and thus superior to the world.

- The second image is of the Church as servant people, serving God in worship and in praise, and serving others in our daily lives and in resisting injustice. In doing so, we love God with all our heart, and our neighbours as ourselves (Mark 12.37–39). This model emphasises that the purpose of the Church is for others, and not for itself or its members. As Dietrich Bonhoeffer writes: 'The Church must share in the secular problems of ordinary human life,

" the purpose of the Church is for others, and not for itself or its members.

not dominating but helping and serving.'[1] This image highlights the mission of the Church as a ministry of reconciliation, and the need for social and political action in Jesus' name for the liberation of those who are oppressed. The danger, however, is that the Church and the gospel become equated only with social action or particular political beliefs, and not also with the gospel message of discipleship in the spiritual life and of the importance of worship and prayer.

- A further image of the Church is as an institution of salvation. In this view, the Church is formed and inspired by the call to be 'salt and light' (Matthew 5.13–14), and to 'make disciples of all nations' (Matthew 28.19). On the one hand, this model emphasises the foundational impulse for mission that the Church ought to possess. On the other hand, however, a focus only upon 'winning souls for Christ' has sometimes led to forms of Church that are authoritarian, spiritually exclusive, and disapproving of all forms of witness and service other than the oral proclamation of the gospel.

- A final image of the Church is as a community of the Spirit. Here, the Church is seen as a sign of the new humanity brought about in Jesus Christ, focused upon spiritual renewal and transformation with the Spirit as 'a seal for the day of redemption' (Ephesians 4.30). Certainly, an emphasis on prayer, meditation and spiritual gifts may lead to a close community with deep personal relationships, an absence of hierarchy and a broad sense of equality. However, this image also runs the risk of seeing the Church as a closed group which sets itself apart from the world and departs from the equally pressing need for social transformation.

No single model is capable of triumphing over the other, although since the beginning of the Church, and in our Church today, there have been communities that have become over-reliant on one particular model. There may instead be a benefit for the Church in viewing itself in a way that more fully reflects this diversity of images within the New Testament.

What does it mean to be a Reformed Church in particular?

Following the Protestant Reformation in Scotland, teaching concerning the Church paid particular heed to the work of John Calvin, as mediated by John Knox. In terms of its organisation, the Church of Scotland developed a 'presbyterian' system of governance by Church courts. This tradition has always held to a 'priesthood of all believers' and encouraged an 'apostolate of the laity', meaning that it recognises the value and contribution of all Church members, ordained and lay. At the same time, the system is not a true democracy: instead, there is rule at local, regional and national level by those who are ordained to office, namely ministers and elders. These are the 'presbyters', taken from the Greek word *presbyteros* – meaning 'elder' – that is commonly used in the New Testament.

Calvin set forth two criteria or 'notes' by which one could recognise the presence of a true Church:

> Wherever we see the Word of God preached purely and listened to, and the sacraments administered according to the institution of Christ, we cannot doubt that a church exists.[2]

The Scots Confession chose to add a third 'note', which was 'ecclesiastical discipline uprightly ministered ... whereby vice is repressed and virtue nourished'.[3] This was to become a defining role of the elders and Kirk Session of a congregation at various points in the history of the Church of Scotland.

1. Dietrich Bonhoeffer, *Letters and Papers from Prison* (New York: Macmillan, 1967), p. 204.
2. John Calvin, *Institutes of the Christian Religion* (Louisville, KY: WJKP, 2006), IV.i.9.
3. Scots Confession 1560, Ch. 18.

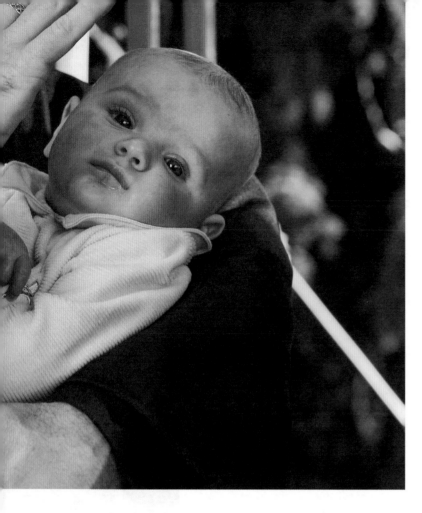

were three kinds of minister: pastors and teachers; those concerned with Church discipline; and deacons to take care of the poor and dispense alms.[4] This translates into the offices of minister, elder and deacon in the present-day Church of Scotland.

How do these Scriptural models and Reformed 'notes' of the Church relate to the claim of the Nicene Creed that we believe in a Church that is 'one, holy, catholic and apostolic'? The answer is that they all should be read as complementary in informing our understanding of what the Church should be.

- As for being 'one', the worldwide Christian Church is clearly not unified institutionally, given its many branches. Instead, the unity of the Church is to be seen in the shared belief in Jesus Christ and commitment to the gospel. Unity can thus be seen in the common impulse of Christians to engage in God's mission, which will seek to re-unite people to each other and to God.

- Unless we are convinced of our own spiritual purity and righteousness, how can we recognise our own imperfect humanity and still call ourselves 'holy'? The Church is 'holy' as it is called and sent by God to speak of God's holiness and not our own, and to act to express God's love for the world. In other words, the Church is 'holy' only in so far as it finds its holiness in Jesus Christ and conforms to God's mission in the world.

- The first Protestant Reformers claimed to be 'catholic' in terms of being a continuation of (and not a departure from) the true Church. Today, however, we may think of the Church as 'catholic' or 'universal' to the extent that each church recognises its connection to other Christians around the globe, and is deliberately inclusive of all genders and ethnicities of people.

- For Darrell Guder, the last note of the Church, that the Church is 'apostolic', should really come first, to indicate an understanding of the Church that is both dynamic and missional.[5] This would reflect more faithfully the idea that every baptised Christian is principally called to live a Christian life in mission, however that mission is shown in their own life and congregation.

A central theme, therefore, of the understanding of the nature of the Church in the Church of Scotland is the presence of Christ through the proclamation of the Word of God – in the reading and preaching of Scripture and in the sacraments – through the work of the Spirit. Calvin – with Luther – considered that there were not seven sacraments (as in the mediaeval Church) but only two – namely baptism and the Lord's Supper. The benefit of these sacraments for the faithful is that they convey God's grace, strengthen belief, enhance the unity of the Church, and reassure us of God's promises.

According to Scripture, God has given God's people 'gifts...that some would be apostles, some evangelists, some pastors and teachers to equip the saints for the work of ministry [and] for building up the body of Christ' (Ephesians 4. 11-12). This understanding of a diversity of roles, combined with the 'notes' of a true Church, in turn required Calvin to define who was responsible for Word and sacrament, and who for governance alone. Calvin concluded from his analysis of the New Testament, in particular of 1 Timothy 5.17, that there

4. Calvin, *Institutes of the Christian Religion*, IV.iv.1.
5. Darrell Guder, 'A Multicultural and Translational Approach', in Craig Ott, ed., *The Mission of the Church: Five Views in Conversation* (Grand Rapids: Baker Academic, 2016), p. 24.

What has the Church done and what should the Church do?

In present-day Scotland, we live in an increasingly secularised society. The presence of a Christian community in the midst of a city, town or country village is still tolerated, but often expected to restrict itself to a private realm of belief. This means that it should not interact with public institutions, in any way impose its own narratives and truth claims upon the liberties of others, or disturb rational and scientific public 'fact'. Expressing faith in our everyday lives has become troublesome, and often socially or legally unacceptable.

We may have partly contributed in the Church to that marginalisation. We played centre stage in a Scottish society before the social revolution of the 1960s where the Church of Scotland wielded much power, privilege and social control at national and local level, assuming that it had a rightful place as moral and spiritual arbiter of the nation. That vision of 'Christendom' has been decisively rejected by society in our present day.

We perhaps emphasised individual salvation to the extent that we lost focus also on the reconciling love of God in building a new community, and the command of Christ that we should act first for others and not ourselves, as a foretaste of God's Kingdom. The consequence was that faith was often severed from the world of the working week, and became a Sunday affair. These social and spiritual factors led to an 'attractional' understanding of the Church: it was expected that people would attend because it was a duty or social habit, and it was considered that mission was a form of 'revivalism' to entice lapsed, baptised Christians 'back to the Church'. In this way, we perhaps failed to see mission instead as the overflowing of the gospel in word and deed within society, and as a task for everyone called by Christ, without the necessity for an institutional purpose or intended gain.

Due to its scale and public position, the Church also became a more bureaucratic organisation, running the risk of being self-serving and internalised, and distant from its true calling and identity as an ever-reforming movement in the world. And in our infighting, sectarianism and schisms, we failed too often to be a 'light of the world', or 'a city built on a hill' (Matthew 5.14). Instead, we seemed to reflect a divorce between the gospel as expressed by Jesus Christ and the actual practice of his followers.

We need to step away from all of those hindrances for the gospel to flourish. However, insofar as we recognise that each of us is flawed, broken and sinful, and insofar as we are all called to seek forgiveness, transformation and salvation in Christ, those shortcomings in the history of the Church may have been inevitable. Maybe they do no more than illustrate our need for God's grace. Our lives as servants of God, and our actions in gathering as a Christian community, will always reflect a mere fraction of his image.

A central motif of the Christian faith, however, is hope. That hope is formed in the expectation that Jesus has inaugurated God's Kingdom in his life, death and resurrection, and that it will be completed and consummated in his coming again into the world. We live in hope of that time when all suffering and strife will end and a new world of peace, justice and reconciliation will be established. In our present tension between the 'now' of the present and the 'not yet' of the time to come, we are called to act decisively in the world towards those ends in the power of the Spirit.

Therefore, at the heart of the future agenda of the Church should be, first, the idea that mission towards those ends is not an occasional function that belongs to the Church and us, but is rather, in the words of Jürgen Moltmann, 'God's activity, which embraces both the Church and world'.[6] This realisation is at the heart of the understanding of the *missio Dei* ('mission of God'), which over the past sixty years has turned upside down ideas of the place of the Church in the world, and the role of the Church in mission.

In line with this thinking, the Church can no longer be a triumphant institution ready to conquer the world around it, but must instead work at a humbler level, as a servant of God. The Church is being sent by God as part of God's mission in the world to further the Kingdom of God: 'there is Church because there is mission, not vice versa'.[7] This mission will take many forms in the world, seeking to offer a prophetic witness in conversation with others.

Second, mission must lie at the core of the Church, and so also of everyone within it, not just its ministers. The Church is the community of those who have been transformed by God's mission. We must, in turn, seek to be agents of further transformation. This is why the Church exists. Mission should not be an occasional function imagined by a small group for a series of events, but should be what defines the Church in all its activity.

However, the purpose of mission is not primarily to increase church numbers, or to preserve the institution. Instead, mission is carried out as a visible and audible expression of God's love for the whole of creation, so that the gospel will come alive in the communities in which we live and work. We do so not for gain, but because God has commanded and sent us to a life of discipleship in mission in a broad sense – proclaiming the gospel, nurturing faith, serving others, challenging injustice and caring for creation.

Therefore, although mission is integral to the Church, and the Church can be a hub for mission to flourish, the Church is not the purpose of mission, or necessarily its end result. The challenge to us all was set out recently by the prominent scholar of Christian mission, Stephen Bevans, who said: 'Mission in Britain and in the secularised West today needs once and for all to recognise that the point of the church is not the church, but the Reign of God.'[8]

mission is carried out as a visible and audible expression of God's love for the whole of creation

6. Jürgen Moltmann, *The Church in the Power of the Spirit* (New York: Harbour Row, 1977), p. 64.
7. David Bosch, *Transforming Mission: Paradigm Shifts in Theology of Mission* (New York: Orbis, 1991), p. 390.
8. Stephen Bevans, 'Mission in Britain Today: Some Modest Reflections and Proposals', *The Journal of Wesley House Cambridge*, Volume 1.2 (2015), pp. 170–1.

QUESTIONS

1. What does it mean to you to be part of the Church?

2. Which of the New Testament models of Church, Calvin's marks of the Church, or the notes of the Church in the Nicene Creed, do you think are important?

3. How should the Church engage in God's mission in the world, and how might you be a part of that mission in sharing the gospel through what you say and do?

Loving and living Lord,
we come to the kirk
to worship You.
Enfolded in stone,
we worship You.
Sheltered from wind and cold,
we worship You.
Embraced by Your Spirit,
we worship You.
Renewed by Your love,
we worship You.
Come, Lord,
turn us around
and send us out
so that the empty space
within these walls
may speak more eloquently
about a people alive in the world
with Your Spirit
of goodness and grace,
peace and reconciliation.

THE CHRISTIAN LIFE

Bible Study: **Alison Jack**

Reflection: **Jan Mathieson**

Prayer: **David D. Scott**

BIBLE STUDY

'Take up your cross daily'
Luke 9.23

Luke 14.11 and 18.14
Philippians 2.8
Luke 5.16 and Luke 22.42
Luke 5.1–11, 27–32
Luke 9.23–27

The Gospel of Luke is very concerned with discipleship. We have more stories about Jesus calling people to join him in this Gospel than in any of the others, and the cost of being a disciple is laid out in the most stark terms. In this Gospel, Jesus is offered as a model for later disciples to follow. Twice he teaches that the exalted will be humbled and the humbled exalted (Luke 14.11 and 18.14; compare Philippians 2.8), and in his life of sacrificial obedience to God, he embodies all that he demands of those who would be his disciples. A man of personal prayer (Luke 5.16), on the eve of his death, Jesus prays: 'Yet not my will but yours be done' (Luke 22.42). Prayerful obedience is the hallmark of discipleship in this Gospel.

In the story that describes the calling of Simon, James and John to discipleship, we have a well-developed narrative with lots of action (Luke 5.1–11). Simon is in the right place to help Jesus, who wants to speak to the crowds from a boat on the lake. After Jesus has finished (and presumably Simon has heard the teaching along with everyone else), he encourages Simon to go into deeper water and put down the nets. To Simon's astonishment, the catch is bigger than the first boat is able to handle, and the second boat is needed. Jesus assures Peter and his companions that they have no need to be afraid, and that they are going to be catching people rather than fish from now on. With remarkable haste, the group return to shore and turn their backs on everything they know in order to follow Jesus.

Compare this story with another about the effect of meeting Jesus: this time, the setting is the office of the tax collector (Luke 5.27–32). Consider some of the differences between Jesus' approach here and Levi's response, and the approach of Jesus in the earlier story and the response of Simon and his friends. Discipleship seems to mean being called in different ways, depending on your starting-point.

Finally, read Jesus' teaching to those who have made the commitment to become his followers (Luke 9.23–27). This is not an easy path, but one with consequences. What might 'take up your cross' mean to Jesus' hearers, and to the first hearers of the gospel? What might it mean to us today? Can you tease out the relationship between being a fisher of people, and not being ashamed of Jesus and his teaching?

What does it mean to be a disciple?

A hymn sung in many churches asks 'Will you come and follow me?'

It is when we answer that question with a 'Yes' that we begin a journey of discipleship, seeking to live in a Christ-like way in our world today.

But what does that involve – *what does it mean to follow Jesus*?

Discipleship demands that we know something of Jesus and so we may want to learn more about the life of Jesus and his teachings which we find in the Gospels. Some may want to go further and explore some of the many works on the historical person of Jesus or on what it means for the Church to say that Jesus is both wholly divine and holy human.

None of these explorations, however, gives us a set of instructions about how to live our Christian lives today. What we do discover are a series of principles or values which we must translate for our own time and situation. We find the example of a way of life lived at one with God, to which we can aspire, but which we cannot copy exactly.

Nor is knowing Jesus merely knowing *about* Jesus. Therefore part of discipleship is the experience of worship, through which we may discover more of God, revealed to us in Jesus Christ. In praise, preaching and prayer we are drawn into the mystery that is God and we can begin to use our minds and experience to work out how we follow the teaching and example of Jesus in our lives, lived now in a very different context.

In his letter to the Galatians, Paul speaks of the kind of behaviour that is unbecoming of Christian disciples and then identifies the nine-fold fruit of the Spirit (Galatians 5.22–23). These qualities are those that the disciples of Jesus are to seek to exhibit. For some, such qualities may come easily, but in other cases we may need to work hard at modifying our speech or our behaviour so that it is more closely modelled on Christ.

In his letters to the Corinthians and Ephesians, Paul further identifies some of the different gifts and abilities that followers of Jesus may have. Here we see that being a disciple is not a solitary pursuit but a communal endeavour. Discipleship commits us to being part of the Church, the body of Christ, 'playing for the team' by using our different gifts to strengthen one another in faith and to build up the Church in which we come together and renew our connection with Christ. The Church is one of the ways in which followers of Jesus both discover and display the kind of life made possible by Christ – a way of living that values the other as well as the self and that acknowledges that life is a gift of God whose Spirit enables us to live that life to the full, rooted in the love we are called to show and share.

If worship is the oxygen of our Christian life and the fellowship of other Christians its life-blood, then its heart-beat is the service that it gives to the world and the peoples within it in the name of Christ.

" what does
it mean
to follow
Jesus?

The prophets of the Old Testament called upon God's people to care for the poor, the weak and the vulnerable. In the Gospels we are told of Jesus' love for the outcast, the stranger, those in need. The parables that Jesus tells reinforce this point, speaking of a divine love that is unconfined and unbound by narrow interpretations, but is instead immeasurable and limitless – a love that recognises no barriers but which draws all people into its embrace.

This is the kind of love that Christian disciples are called to put into action, sometimes at great cost. The teacher and pastor Dietrich Bonhoeffer, put to death for his opposition to the Nazi regime, reminds us that there is no such thing as 'cheap grace' and speaks instead of 'costly grace'. Such sacrificial service lives on in many forms in the Church today. We find individuals and congregations providing breakfast clubs for children, foodbanks for the hungry, street pastors, support for refugees, care for those suffering from conditions like dementia, or transport to hospital appointments for the infirm. Some may argue – rightly – that such humanitarian service can be given by those who are not Christian. The difference is not in the compassion shown or the assistance given but in its motivation. We offer such service *in the name of Jesus Christ* whose we are and whom we serve (cf. Acts 27.23). It is part of a life of discipleship.

Being a disciple of Jesus also encourages us to have a wider perspective. Service is not just offered to those around us or those who live the same kind of life as we do. It involves us making ourselves aware of the needs of others, whom we may never know, who live out their lives far away from us. So individuals and church congregations support organisations such as Christian Aid with its many development projects around the world, and the Church of Scotland HIV/Aids project which delivers education, care and support both locally and in Africa. They also support the work of mission partners and partner churches overseas, who are helping to build relationships and promote peace in places of desperate conflict or serving in refugee camps and detention centres in Europe and beyond. Such support is not simply financial but also takes the form of an ongoing commitment to prayer.

We live in a time when we must face many ethical questions that could not have been imagined in the time of Jesus. Climate change and our response to it is something we must consider today, and discipleship means looking to God in Christ in order to shape our attitude and response as we are challenged and empowered to care for the earth. Scientific advances bring other challenges to us, and we must bring our Christian faith to bear on many new matters – from genetic research to end-of-life issues. It is important to acknowledge that Christians may hold different views on these matters. But the dialogue between science and faith is one in which we must engage in a respectful, informed and faithful manner.

It is sometimes said that the Church should not 'dabble' in politics, yet it is impossible to live a life of discipleship and not concern ourselves with the way in which society is ordered. The life of Jesus gives an example of promoting justice and equality, of seeking peace and of standing up for what is right. For some, discipleship will mean engaging directly in political or public life, speaking truth to power, and for all Christian disciples the faithful life will involve resisting those things that diminish life and promoting those things that allow all people to live lives of integrity, knowing God's blessing on them.

Sometimes reluctance to embark and continue on a life of Christian discipleship arises because we think that we need to have worked out in advance all the answers to the difficult situations that arise in life, whether the awkward questions we may be asked about our faith or the adverse challenges we may face in our own experience or with which others may confront us. Yet it is only *through* a life of discipleship that we may find some of these answers. It is through following Jesus and living life in relationship with God that we discover more about God and about being human.

The new perspective this journey of discipleship opens up is one that extends beyond the horizon of our mortal life. To be a disciple of Jesus is to share the hope he gives us that the life we are living is eternal life: the life of God in which we share now and which also endures beyond time and space. Thus to follow Jesus is to travel ever closer to the heart of God and, in so doing, to find ourselves and to find meaning and purpose in our lives.

The demand 'Will you come and follow me?' is therefore not so much a question as a calling. It is the vocation of every Christian disciple – the unique lifestyle and unique quality of life that we discover through following Jesus and that we display to the world as, together, we journey with him, in faith and in discipleship, in and for the world today.

66 to follow Jesus is to travel ever closer to the heart of God

What is the point of prayer?

OMG!

The letters scream at us from celebrity magazines and text messages, from social media posts and countless conversations overheard on trains, in coffee shops and on the streets: OMG!

'O my God!' has become an exclamation of astonishment or distress, a cry for attention or of alarm. And perhaps it has always been so – for 'O my God!' is the most basic form of prayer.

Prayer is our communication with something or someone beyond ourselves: in prayer we express our deepest feelings and fears, our most worrying doubts and our most intense longings and happiness.

'OMG!' is a prayer that comes to us from the pages of Scripture.

In the book of Psalms the writer calls out to God in a range of different circumstances, reflecting a whole gamut of emotions and experiences: from 'Bless the Lord, O my soul' (Psalm 103.1) through 'I waited patiently for the Lord' (Psalm 40.1) to the more angry and agitated 'Do not be silent, O God of my praise' (Psalm 109.1). Sometimes, as the writer thinks on God, there is an expression of adoration in the face of God's greatness displayed in the world and known in human experience; sometimes that same sense of God's greatness results in a heartfelt plea for forgiveness as human failing and wrongdoing come into focus. The prayers of the psalmist express a relationship with God that is living, changing and multi-faceted.

The same is true of the prayers of Jesus. Here we discover a working out of his relationship with God and a simultaneous exploration of his own identity. In his prayer for his friends and followers, we see an intimate, assured relationship with God: 'protect them in your name that you have given me, so that they may be one, as we are one' (John 17.1). Later, on the cross, there is an expression of anguish and abandonment, together with a plea for understanding: 'My God, my God, why have you forsaken me?' (Matthew 27.46). The Gospels also mention without further detail other times at which Jesus withdraws to pray alone – in the wilderness or on the mountain-top or at the sea-shore or indoors.

From Jesus we also have instruction on how to pray – and how not to pray – together with the example of prayer we call the Lord's Prayer. Instruction about and an example of prayer is also found in the New Testament letters, helping early Christians and emerging churches engage in prayer and develop in their relationship with God by the power of the Spirit. So Paul enjoins Christians, 'Devote yourselves to prayer' (Colossians 4.1) and encourages them to pray for the churches, for preachers, for peace, for world and civic leaders, and for one another – as well as for their own personal concerns (Philippians 4.6). And we read, for example in Acts, of prayers being made by a whole range of people in a wide variety of places from their homes through prison cells to public squares.

As Christians today what can we learn from all of this about the place and function of prayer in our faith life – what is the point of prayer?

If we use prayer as a kind of shopping list on our regular visit to God then it is likely that we are going to be disappointed in the results of our prayers and that we will feel that prayer itself is pointless. If we think of prayer as a way to persuade God to have a change of mind, then it is likely that we are going to consider it largely ineffective, making no difference to God or to ourselves. Yet clearly prayer has some value otherwise we would stop praying!

On one level, prayer is when we press the pause button in the midst of our everyday lives. Sometimes that will be in the midst of a crisis and sometimes at a time of overwhelming happiness; sometimes it will be when we do not like ourselves very much and sometimes when we are angry and direct that anger to God. We pause and we pray, taking time and making effort, deliberately seeking to know the sense of God with us. Prayer is therefore deliberate communication with God, the One who is beyond us and yet intimately with us at the same time, even when sometimes we feel that God is absent from us.

In the activity of prayer we re-align our frame of reference – 'not what I want but what you want' (Matthew 26.39) – and we enlarge our vision and our thinking to let them take part in what God is doing. Prayer may lead towards understanding, or towards acceptance, or towards action. Prayer is, then, a human act, in which we seek to engage with God. And through prayer, we may come to realise the qualities we need to model in our own lives to contribute to the outcomes for which we pray.

As we pray for the suffering peoples and places of the world we do not simply give God a set of instructions. We express our desire to see the effects of God's reign established in our world and we may come to see what we can do to contribute to that process. As we pray for healing for ourselves or for others, we entertain the possibility that healing may be more than physical

'O my God!' is the most basic form of prayer.

or psychological restoration, that it may include a deep peace and life-giving hope that comes from the sense that God has our best interests at heart – that he cares not just for our bodies or minds but for our whole selves without limit of time. As we pray for our planet and those with whom we share it we do not simply express our fears and our desires, we may also sense our interconnectedness with all that God has made.

At the same time, prayer is also a context in which we ask God to act and in which God does act. Christians pray to God in the confidence that when they pray in accord with the will of God they will be heard (1 John 5.14) and will obtain their requests (1 John 5.15). Certainly, the answer that God gives to our prayers is perhaps not so often or so much the obvious, simple granting of our wishes and requests. Discerning how God answers our prayers may be part of our broader journey of participating in the divine life of God. In this ongoing and prayerful walk, we will receive new perspective and motivation for our lives, a new understanding of who we are and who we can become, a growing sense of the mystery of our existence in relationship with God and of how God is working in us and in the world. And even when we feel that our prayers are not being heard or answered, Scripture encourages us not to give up on prayer (Luke 18.1).

Prayer is not always easy. Some people find it helpful to have some ritual associated with their prayer life. Some will light a candle, while others will look at something beautiful, while some will hold a particular object or make particular gestures. Many will set aside a particular and regular time for prayer. Some will prepare for prayer by reading a passage of Scripture or a poem or from a prayer book; others prefer a time of silent contemplation. Some will speak their prayers aloud, while others will be silent. And for others yet, prayer can take form in writing or singing or painting. In all cases, prayer is conversation with God and so involves us in listening and in discerning God.

Our private prayer may (or may not) be rather different from the prayer in which we participate publicly, in a church service for example. In the latter, the person leading the prayer may well use a stylised form of words – traditional or modern – in trying to reflect the concerns of the gathered community, expressing their shared concerns while leaving space also for particular requests.

Whether prayer is public or private, we can approach God directly, needing no intermediary except Christ. Thus we pray in the name of Jesus who is our gateway to God. Often, our prayers reflect our understanding of God as Trinity, and so we acknowledge that Jesus Christ is one with God the Father and God the Spirit. Again, whether prayer is public or private, we often use the word 'Amen' to end our prayers. This word has ancient roots and means 'so be it' or 'truly'. This allows us a moment to reflect on what we have said to God and on our sincerity and devotion in saying it.

From 'OMG!' to 'Amen!', prayer gives us a 'time out', allowing us to touch base with God in order better to be able to continue our journey of faith and discipleship.

QUESTIONS

1. What gifts can you identify in yourself and in others that might be used to serve God in the Church and/or in the world today, and how might they be cultivated?

2. How many different moods and expressions of prayer in the Psalms strike a chord with you, and which of these would you wish to communicate to God now?

3. Which figures of discipleship and prayer inspire you in your journey as a disciple, and how might you follow a path on your journey of faith that follows in their footsteps?

Great and glorious God,
we give You thanks
that You have created the Universe
and given it dimension and design.
You have created us in Your own image
and given us a unique vocation
to glorify You and to enjoy Your company for ever.
Through Your Son, Jesus Christ,
You have revealed
the quality and extent of Your love for us –
forgiving the sinner,
healing the broken body,
suffering and dying and rising again
to offer us the gift of eternal life.
By the power of Your Spirit,
You have called us together
to be the body of Christ
and given us a variety of gifts
to share this glorious gospel
that the people of the earth
may live in the Kingdom of Heaven.
Enable us
to treasure Your Word within our hearts,
listen prayerfully to Your Spirit,
taste the bread of Your undying love
and live and work for Your praise and glory
that at the end of all our days
we may enter into the joy
of Your heavenly company
through Jesus Christ, our Lord,
who lives and reigns with You and the Spirit,
ever one God, now and for evermore.

THE HEAVENLY THINGS

Bible Study:	Alison Jack
Reflection:	Andrew Torrance
Prayer:	David D. Scott

BIBLE STUDY

'We will all be changed'
1 Corinthians 15.51

Genesis 37.35
Psalm 138.7–8
1 Kings 1.21
Luke 16.19–31
1 Corinthians 15.35–55
John 14.1–4

There are many different word pictures offered in the Bible to describe the mystery that is heaven.

In the Old Testament, there seems to be a general belief that everyone will go to the same place after death, a place called Sheol. This is usually translated as 'hell', or the 'grave', or sometimes by the Greek term 'Hades'. Even the Patriarchs of the Old Testament expect to end up here when they die. When Jacob is told his son is dead, he mourns by asserting that he will 'go down to Sheol to my son' (Genesis 37.35). Crucially, though, this is a place where God is, rather than a place of separation from him, or a place associated with Satan/the Devil (see Psalm 138.7–8: 'If I make my bed in Sheol, you are there!'). Death is associated with sleep rather than punishment, so Bathsheba explains King David's death as a time 'when my lord the king sleeps with his fathers' (1 Kings 1.21).

In the New Testament, there is a more complicated set of word pictures offered to describe what is ultimately unknown. For one word picture, read the parable of the Rich Man and Lazarus (Luke 16.19–31). Does the parable give any clues about what leads to one place rather than another after death? Consider what the purpose of this parable might be, and how this may affect the picture of life after death it presents.

For another word picture, expressed in a very different genre, read 1 Corinthians 15.35–49. Earlier in this chapter, Christ's resurrection is described as changing everything. He is the 'first fruits of those who have died', without which 'our proclamation has been in vain' (verse 14). The timing of the general resurrection of the dead is uncertain, in this passage, but the extreme contrast between the earthly and the heavenly is heavily emphasised with the use of a series of opposites. Do some of these speak more helpfully to you than others?

Finally, Jesus in John's Gospel offers a very concrete word picture for heaven. In John 14.1–4, Jesus describes the place where God is (his 'house') as having many dwelling-spaces for those to whom he is speaking. More than this – these spaces are prepared by Jesus, and he will take his hearers there. The picture is deliberately domestic, designed to bring peace to the troubled. It works together with Paul's confident assertion that 'When this perishable body puts on imperishability, and this mortal body puts on immortality, then the saying that is written will be fulfilled: "Death has been swallowed up in victory"' (1 Corinthians 15.54).

What is heaven like?

Amid the challenges of this world, heaven tends to be viewed as a source of hope. It offers the prospect of a better world characterised by overwhelming joy and flourishing, a world untainted by the evil and suffering we witness today. For example, it is sometimes envisioned as a paradise that awaits us in the distant future. It is easy to imagine heaven as a sunny beach, margarita in hand, the shade of a palm tree, and Bob Marley playing live in the background. Or perhaps it is a wonderland in the clouds, resplendent with the voices of angels singing, and cherubs playing lyres – which may beg the question, 'will I get bored in heaven?'

There are elements of truth in both of these images, in the peace, joy and beauty they depict. But they are also very far from adequate. Not only do they present heaven as a place of escape from this world, they also have little to do with God. When Christian teaching about heaven focuses on the location of the afterlife, it is very easy for God to end up being sidelined. God can easily come to be viewed merely as the means of our getting into heaven – an extra who will hang around with those who make it there. But that is to miss the point.

When it comes to a Christian view of heaven, it is God who must be seen as the focal point. God is the One who makes heaven what it is. Moreover, it is God who defines what human flourishing will be like in heaven. In heaven, God is 'all in all' (1 Corinthians 15.28). In the brokenness of this world, we can only just begin to fathom such things.

So how is such fathoming possible at all? It is possible because heaven is not simply a transcendent reality, beyond the horizon of this world. There are ways in which heavenly realities are communicated to us in this world. For example, heavenly flourishing not only awaits us in the future, as an unfathomable surprise that will burst into our lives after death. By being drawn into a life of faith in the present, we can get a glimpse of what heaven is really like as we grow into our heavenly lives in this world.

To think about the heavenly life in this world requires us to ask about what it means to live before God, in the lives for which we were created and, more broadly, in the creation for which we were created. When we reflect on this, we find that a Christian understanding needs not only to relate to the Christian view of hope but also to the Christian practice of discipleship – and so to speak to us of what it means to discover and, further, to live into our true humanity.

How does heaven relate to creation?

In Scripture, heaven is portrayed in many ways. But it is perhaps most commonly presented as the transcendent realm in which God is most fully present. It is the realm under and before which creation was created to exist; creatures were created to repose in the presence of God and to be formed by this presence.

But creation has failed to reach this end. So, for most of the Bible, we are presented with a story of reconciliation: the story of God bringing creation out of exile, back into the fullness of right relationship with its Creator – back into God's heavenly presence. This story, however, is not about our transcending or escaping our finitude or createdness of our own accord. At the heart of this story is instead the act of God coming to be with us, in and through the person of Jesus Christ. As the apostle Paul writes, 'in Christ God was reconciling the world to himself' (2 Corinthians 5.19).

66 When it comes to a Christian view of heaven, it is God who must be seen as the focal point.

This is the ministry of reconciliation, and it is grounded in two movements:

- The God-humanward, or heaven-creationward movement: Jesus Christ, the Son of God, descends from heaven to be with us in this world – God's heavenly presence becomes one with us in this world. *In Christ, heaven participates in the existence of creation.*

- The human-Godward, or creation-heavenward movement. Following his life, death and resurrection, Jesus Christ ascends to heaven, taking our humanity with him in a movement from humanity to God. In and through the ascension, Jesus Christ perfects our humanity, not simply by taking it to himself but also by presenting it anew to our Father in heaven. So, in and through Christ, humanity is taken home into the loving embrace of the one true source of life: the triune God. *In Christ, creation participates in his heavenly existence.*

In and through these two movements, creation is renewed so that, again in Paul's words, 'if anyone is in Christ, there is a new creation: everything old has passed away; see, everything has become new!' (2 Corinthians 5.17).

So how does this bear on our day-to-day living in this world? When Jesus Christ walked the earth, the heavenly realm shone into this world and set the world alight – 'I [Jesus] am the light of the world. Whoever follows me will never walk in darkness but will have the light of life' (John 8.12). This continues today, albeit differently. Today, the heavenly light of Christ shines into this world through the power of the Spirit. In and through the Spirit, Jesus Christ is present with us. And, in and through the Spirit, we are invited to share in the heavenly life of Christ; we are invited to experience our humanity as it has been united with God in heaven. As this happens – in and through our being reborn from above (John 3.3) – we become empowered to live into a life of loving communion with our heavenly Father and we glimpse that form of human flourishing for which creation was originally purposed and which characterises the heavenly realm.

But the Spirit 'blows where it chooses' (John 3.8), and the Spirit is yet to awaken the whole of creation to live in the light of its heavenly glory. Much of the world remains blind to the radiance of Jesus Christ, the One who makes all things new (Revelation 21.5). It does not yet know that the new creation has dawned, and continues to exist as if nothing has happened, remaining lost in the shadows.

To transform this situation, to continue to draw the world out of the shadows, the Spirit does not work alone. Rather, the Spirit enlivens a community to share in the ministry of reconciliation as it lives as the body of Christ in this world. This is the role of the Church – to seek to live as God's Kingdom come, where God's will is done, on earth as it is heaven.

To associate heaven with the Church can seem strange. The congregations of this world always fall short of their heavenly calling. But, for the Church, crumbling congregations can never shake its one true cornerstone. From heaven, Jesus not only sends the Spirit to give form to the Church in this world. He also lives as the great high priest who continually intercedes for us (Hebrews 4.14–16). So, when we fall short of our createdness, when we fall short of being who we truly are and are called to be, we can know that our humanity is represented by the One who loves us more than we can love ourselves. We are not made right with God by our works, but by the loving faithfulness of Jesus Christ, upon whom the faith of the Church is grounded (cf. Romans 8.31–39).

When God calls to us 'from above', by the sending of the Spirit, God does not call us to find our own way out of the wilderness. God makes us witnesses to the resurrection of Jesus so that 'we too might walk in newness of life' (Romans 6.4). By learning of the resurrection, we learn that we have been delivered out of the wilderness. The resurrection directs our eyes to the living person of Christ – the one mediator between God and humanity (1 Timothy 2.5) – in whom creation *is*, already, at one with God. And we are invited to enjoy fellowship with God by participating in the new creation and the new humanity inaugurated by him.

Jesus Christ is therefore the only way that creation participates in a heavenly life, and he is the only one who is our heavenly hope. The hope of heaven is thus not most immediately the hope of a new world that awaits us after death, if we 'succeed' at 'Christianity'. The immediate hope of heaven lies in the One who calls us to himself so that we might catch sight of heaven today – Jesus Christ, whose life is the promise of our heavenly life.

What is heaven like on earth?

The phrase 'heaven on earth' is often used to describe a scene of visible beauty. But, from a Christian perspective, 'heaven on earth' is much more than that. It is not simply a place that satisfies our aesthetic sensibilities. It is that particular space that is defined by the shape of the body of Christ and by the outpouring of the Spirit, so that those who share in the space might learn what it means to give glory to our Father, who art in heaven and to whom we pray 'Thy Kingdom come ...'

But what might this space look like to us in this world?

The first thing to note about heaven on earth is that it is not a kingdom that can be immediately experienced. As Jesus says to the Pharisees, 'The Kingdom of God is not coming with things that can be observed.' The Kingdom will not be so obvious that people shout, 'Look, here it is!' or 'There it is!' To participate in God's Kingdom, a person needs to be given the eyes to see that 'the Kingdom of God is among you' (cf. Luke 17.20–21).

To glimpse God's Kingdom requires faith in the One who is God's Kingdom come – Jesus Christ. Heaven on earth is where the earth reflects the fact that God is with us; it is where the Spirit is awakening persons to correspond to the presence of Jesus Christ.

But, as we have already intimated, in this world, the new creation is surrounded by the old. The heavenly life is surrounded by death and destruction. Nowhere is this more evident than in the fact that, when the fullness of heavenly reality dwelt among us, he was crucified. So, when we lead heavenly lives in this world, Scripture warns us, we will be led into persecution. When God's Kingdom comes to earth, those who participate in this Kingdom will find themselves living in a way that goes against the grain of this world. To the secular world, it will almost be as though Christians are living their lives ***as if*** they were living in a different world. This is because the sinful world is not the natural habitat for the heavenly life. As Jesus said, 'My Kingdom is not from this world' (John 18.36).

Heaven on (the old) earth looks very different from (the new) earth in heaven.

But, as we have also intimated, although the heavenly light of Christ is surrounded by darkness, the darkness does not overcome it. Death has been overcome by the power of resurrection. So, today, Christians can live in the hope of the heavenly life that has been established. To live in this hope is to live into the life of the Church; it is to follow Jesus Christ and share in the life of his body.

What happens when heaven comes to earth – when Jesus is present in this world? The hungry are fed, the thirsty are given something to drink, the stranger is welcomed, the naked are clothed, the prisoner is visited, and the secular world hears the gospel (Matthew 25.34–40). Why? Because when the Kingdom comes, we are conformed to the person of Christ, and so we serve to make these things happen.

But, to be clear, this outreach is not about Christians bringing heaven to those in need. Rather, for Christians, it is a pilgrimage of going to where heaven is to be found in this world, to where Christ is to be found. It is here that we belong. When God's Kingdom comes, our heavenly flourishing finds natural and unselfconscious expression in our serving the earthly flourishing of the marginalised, the poor, the suffering, the secular. This is because our heavenly flourishing looks to their earthly flourishing, and finds expression in their earthly flourishing. Heavenly flourishing is intertwined with earthly flourishing. When 'we love one another, God lives in us' (1 John 4.12). Heaven on earth is a space where earthly flourishing is created by way of heavenly flourishing.

How will I know if I am going to heaven?

It is common for heaven to be presented as a reward for good behaviour and good beliefs. Undergirding this view is an idea of God as making heaven possible for us but, to some extent, leaving it up to us to make the decisive contribution that will determine whether or not we go to heaven when we die.

It is normally with this kind of vision in mind that a person will ask the anxious question 'How will I know if I am going to heaven?' or, indeed, 'How do I know that my loved ones will be going to heaven?' The anxiety of these questions is often compounded by images of hell as an eternal chamber of torment that has been prepared for those who fail to believe or act adequately in this world.

Not only is this vision perhaps confused; it can even become dangerous. It has enormous potential to encourage a life of discipleship that is primarily oriented towards a self-interested hope of paradise and driven by a fear of eternal suffering. And where would God be in such a vision? God would primarily be viewed as the One who sends persons one way or the other – either up or down. And this would mean that God would primarily be viewed as a means to an end.

On this view, the question 'How will I know if I am going to heaven?' becomes 'How will I know that God is going to let me into heaven?'

The simple answer to this question is: 'God loves you more than you love yourself and wants nothing more than to embrace you into eternal fellowship.' And what about the person who does not believe in God? To that question, the answer is the same. God loves each and every one of us unconditionally, regardless of the extent to which a person might know and respond to this fact. Scripture tells us that God 'desires everyone to be saved and to come to the knowledge of the truth' (1 Timothy 2.4). This means that the question of a person's eternal destiny is one that is best entrusted to God. The Christian does not primarily hope for heaven but hopes instead in the God who 'is love' (1 John 4.8).

God loves each and every one of us unconditionally

Knowing the love of God, as it is revealed in Jesus Christ, inspires not only hope for the Christian world but hope for all things (Colossians 1.20). Jesus Christ is the only way to heaven, and he opens the doors for the whole of creation to participate in the heavenly life that awaits it.

Does this mean that everyone is going to heaven? Again, this may be the wrong question to ask and may even miss the point. The question about our ultimate destiny should always focus on God as the One to whom we all belong, and is not a question that we are ever in a place to answer for ourselves. Instead, it is one that we must entrust to God, whose love

> was revealed among us in this way: God sent his only Son into the world so that we might live through him. In this is love, not that we loved God but that he loved us and sent his Son to be the atoning sacrifice for our sins. (1 John 4.9–10)

There is nothing more, nothing greater or more hopeful that can be said here.

So, when it comes to issues regarding the number of people in heaven or hell, we need to proceed with what the tradition has sometimes described as a 'holy silence'. Why be silent at this point? Because the goal of the Christian life is not primarily a particular celestial destination but **fellowship with God**, and this requires us to trust and hallow the triune God whose hands are over our situation in ways that we must entrust to God.

When we understand matters in this way, our attention can return to focusing on more immediate matters. The question 'How will I know if I am going to heaven?' will be displaced by the questions 'How can I live in the light of heaven today?' and 'How can I ensure that my neighbour can glimpse the Kingdom through me?' If a person is, for some reason, prioritising the former question over the latter, it is possible that they are missing out on the full extent of what heaven truly is, and how it truly relates to this world.

QUESTIONS

1. In what way does this chapter challenge some popular ideas of what heaven is like?

2. What are some examples of church practices that reflect God's Kingdom come on earth, as it is in heaven?

3. How might we best give hope to someone who has lost a loved one who was not a Christian?

Lord of beginnings
let us begin
with confidence
and in faith
that You go with us.
Lord of endings
let us finish
with good grace
and our loyalty to You
undiminished.
Lord of the journey
let us travel
in the faith
that our ending
may not be the end of the journey
and our task
may not be to see the journey done
but to enable others to see
what we have never seen
and to enjoy
what we have never enjoyed
save through the promises
of Jesus Christ,
our Saviour and Lord.

Further Reading

There are a number of resources available which would allow you to continue to explore the Christian faith. An initial list of suggestions for further reading is given below, ordered by the themes of the preceding sections.

Knowing God
Burgess, John P., *Why Scripture Matters*, Louisville: Westminster John Knox Press, 1998.
McGrath, Alister E., *Christian Theology: An Introduction*, 5th edn, Oxford: Blackwell, 2011, Ch. 6.
Migliore, Daniel L., *Faith Seeking Understanding: An Introduction to Christian Theology*, 3rd edn, Grand Rapids: Eerdmans, 2014 , Chs 2 and 3.

God the Creator
Bauckham, Richard, *Bible and Ecology: Rediscovering the Community of Creation*, London: Darton, Longman and Todd, 2010.
Fergusson David A. S., *Creation*, Grand Rapids: Eerdmans, 2014.
McGrath, Alister E., *Science and Religion: A New Introduction*, Oxford: Wiley-Blackwell, 2011.

God the Saviour
Bockmuehl, Markus (ed.), *The Cambridge Companion to Jesus*, Cambridge: Cambridge University Press, 2001.
Plantinga, Richard J., Thomas R. Thompson and Matthew D. Lundberg, *An Introduction to Christian Theology*, Cambridge: Cambridge University Press, 2010, Chs 9 and 10.
Spence, Alan J., *Christology: A Guide for the Perplexed*, London: Continuum/T&T Clark, 2008.

God the Spirit
Castelo, Daniel, *Pneumatology: A Guide for the Perplexed*, London: Bloomsbury, 2015.
Kärkkäinen, Veli-Matti, *Spirit and Salvation: The Sources of Christian Theology*, Louisville: Westminster John Knox Press, 2010.
Plantinga, Richard J., Thomas R. Thompson and Matthew D. Lundberg, *An Introduction to Christian Theology*, Cambridge: Cambridge University Press, 2010, Ch. 11.

The Christian Church
Hirst, Alan and Michael Frost, *The Shaping of Things to Come: Innovation and Mission for the 21st-Century Church*, Grand Rapids: Baker Books, 2013.
Migliore, Daniel L., *Faith Seeking Understanding: An Introduction to Christian Theology*, 3rd edn, Grand Rapids: Eerdmans, 2014, Ch. 11.
Ott, Craig (ed.), *The Mission of the Church: Five Views in Conversation*, Grand Rapids: Baker Academic, 2016.

The Christian Life
Bonhoeffer, Dietrich, *The Cost of Discipleship*, London: SCM Press, 1959.
Foster, Richard, *Prayer: Finding the Heart's True Home*, London: Hodder & Stoughton, 2008.
Nouwen, Henri J. M., *The Wounded Healer*, London: Darton, Longman and Todd, 2014.

The Heavenly Things
Farrow, Douglas, *Ascension Theology*, London: T&T Clark, 2011.
McKnight, Scot, *The Heaven Promise: Engaging the Bible Truth about Life to Come*, London: Hodder & Stoughton, 2015.
Wright, N. T., *Simply Good News*, New York: HarperOne, 2015.

LIST OF CONTRIBUTORS

David Fergusson is Professor of Divinity and Principal of New College at the University of Edinburgh.

Alexander (Sandy) Forsyth teaches Practical Theology at the University of Glasgow, and is Associate Minister at Bearsden Cross Parish Church.

Frances Henderson is Minister of Hoddom, Kirtle-Eaglesfield and Middlebie Parish Church.

Alison Jack is Senior Lecturer in New Testament and Assistant Principal of New College at the University of Edinburgh.

Jan Mathieson is Minister of Williamwood Parish Church.

Paul T. Nimmo is King's Professor of Systematic Theology at the University of Aberdeen.

Sarah Lane Ritchie is Research Fellow in Theology and Science at the University of St Andrews.

David D. Scott is Minister in the Parish of Traprain.

Andrew Torrance is Lecturer in Theology at the University of St Andrews.